Art
for the Public

Art for the Public

THE COLLECTION OF THE PORT AUTHORITY OF NEW YORK AND NEW JERSEY

PUBLISHED BY THE PORT AUTHORITY

Essays by

DOROTHY C. MILLER
Senior Curator Emeritus
of Painting and Sculpture
The Museum of Modern Art, New York

SAM HUNTER
Professor
Department of Art and Archaeology
Princeton University

OF NEW YORK AND NEW JERSEY

FRONT COVER:
George Segal
The Commuters. 1980
Bronze with white patina (cast 1981),
84" x 72" x 96"
Port Authority Bus Terminal

FRONTISPIECE AND BACK COVER:
Alexander Calder
Flight (.125). 1957
Painted-steel mobile, 45' wide x 17' diameter
John F. Kennedy International Airport,
International Arrivals Building

THE PORT AUTHORITY OF NY & NJ

Copyright © 1985 The Port Authority of New York and New Jersey
Published by The Port Authority of New York and New Jersey
One World Trade Center
New York, N.Y. 10048

Designed by Leon Auerbach Design Associates
Edited by Jane Fluegel
Additional research by Barbara Ross
Type set by Graphic Technology Inc.
Printed by Howard Press Inc.
Printed in the United States of America

Library of Congress Catalog Card Number 83-620026
ISBN 0-914773-00-3

This book is published with the aid of
generous grants from Mrs. Charles W. Engelhard
and Lila Acheson Wallace

Contents

Joan Miró
World Trade Center
Tapestry. 1974
Wool and hemp, 20' x 35'
Two World Trade Center
(Mezzanine)

Alan Sagner at unveiling of Louise Nevelson's *Sky Gate, New York*, One World Trade Center, 1978. Seated are Nevelson, left, and Kitty Carlisle Hart, Chairman, New York State Council on the Arts

Foreword

ALAN SAGNER
Chairman
Board of Commissioners
The Port Authority
of New York
and New Jersey

A public agency that builds large shapes in larger spaces is inescapably involved in aesthetics. The span of the George Washington Bridge soars out of the Palisades rock, the Bayonne arch looks pure against the western sky. To the driver the bridges are but land-to-land crossings over water, their function outweighing their form. Yet if there is beauty in the shape and placement of the bridges, they approach the domain of art.

To leave aesthetics to accident and abide by the rules of function alone is to waste an important public opportunity. Cramped buildings and boxlike offices dedicated to bare economic necessity crab the public spirit, whereas spaces and shapes dedicated to the human spirit are an encouragement, expanding the will.

The Port Authority of New York and New Jersey regards the airports, bridges and tunnels, the World Trade Center, the terminals, containerports, industrial enterprises, and rail transit system in its care as landmarks, and attempts to upgrade them over the years not only to maintain superior levels of service but also to preserve them as authentic regional symbols. Going beyond function, a Port Authority engineer sets aesthetic standards in designing a ramp over a highway with a unique and lovely curve; a Port Authority environmentalist seeks the rare right combination of plants to do the work of containing the noise and fumes of a toll plaza. The Port Authority considers enrichment of the region's quality of life to be a fundamental obligation, whether in the generation of hundreds of millions of dollars to fund new projects or in the planting of a flower border at the approach to a bridge. The obligation extends to the encouragement of an investment in public art.

With the help of our knowledgeable and devoted Committee on Art, the Port Authority has sought to marry contemporary art to its own contemporary functions. New art has been commissioned and the work of contemporary artists acquired, all at a cost well below the guidelines set by law and practice in the states of New York and New Jersey. The collection, begun in 1969 and cataloged here, is now valued, along with a few precious gifts and grants, at well over four times the original purchase price. The catalog is commended to the public with pride, as evidence of the Port Authority's unlimited desire and persistent endeavor to enrich the quality of life in the region of New York and New Jersey that it serves.

Saul Wenegrat, artist
James Rosati, structural
engineer John Skilling,
and architect Minoru
Yamasaki confer on
placement of Rosati's
Ideogram, 1974, in World
Trade Center plaza

Preface

SAUL S. WENEGRAT
Secretary to the
Committee on Art
The Port Authority
of New York
and New Jersey

The New York-New Jersey metropolitan area is universally recognized as the arts capital of the world. Art in all its forms holds a unique place in the consciousness and economy of the region. More than nineteen hundred arts institutions educate and provide enjoyment annually to over sixty-four million people, thirteen million of whom are visitors from outside the region. The arts are an industry that in 1982 was worth almost six billion dollars to the regional economy. In recent years the arts have become a larger regional employer than the advertising and the computer and data-processing industries. In 1982, the arts generated two billion dollars in personal income and created employment for over one hundred and seventeen thousand men and women.

Visitors who come to the region specifically for its cultural life add one billion, three hundred million dollars to the economy in other expenditures during their stay. The great majority enter through Port Authority facilities—Kennedy, Newark, or LaGuardia airports; the Port Authority Bus Terminal; or, if they drive, one of the Hudson River crossings.

Since the late sixties, the Port Authority has been aware of the arts' growing importance to the region and has tried to assist in their growth and development. Working with organizations and agencies such as the New Jersey State Council on the Arts, the Lower Manhattan Cultural Council, the Musicians Development Fund, the Public Art Fund, The Municipal Art Society, and the 42nd Street Redevelopment Corporation, the Port Authority has provided space and funding for exhibitions and performances, and assisted individual artists, performing groups, and arts institutions. It collaborated with the 42nd Street Redevelopment Corporation, for example, in its efforts to revitalize the Broadway and Off Broad-

way theaters and provide housing for performing artists. Through the Lower Manhattan Cultural Council, the Port Authority has supported art exhibitions and performances at the World Trade Center and throughout lower Manhattan. Through the New Jersey State Council on the Arts, it has sponsored exhibitions by New Jersey artists at the Port Authority Bus Terminal, the World Trade Center, and Newark International Airport.

The Port Authority has taken the initiative in other ways. It transformed office space into artists' studios and an exhibition gallery in its New York Truck Terminal, located in the SoHo area of Manhattan. It has been the host at the World Trade Center and the New York City Passenger Ship Terminal for two New York City Avant-Garde Art Festivals. It provides space at the World Trade Center for the New York Theatre Development Fund to sell half-price tickets daily for Broadway and Off Broadway shows. In collaboration with the Cultural Assistance Center, Inc., the Port Authority documented the importance of the arts to the area and published its findings in 1983 in *The Arts as an Industry: Their Economic Importance to the New York-New Jersey Metropolitan Region.*

The Port Authority further supports the artist through its art-in-architecture program, adopted in 1969, which assigns up to one percent of the construction cost of a public project for art. *Art for the Public* catalogs the art-in-architecture program, a source of major sculpture, murals, paintings, and tapestries on public display in the region's airports, the World Trade Center, and bus, rail, and ship terminals.

The Port Authority's art acquisition policy is similar to that of other progressive governmental agencies and private corporations in the New York-New Jersey Metropolitan Region and elsewhere in the United States. The State of New Jersey by law authorizes the allocation for art of one and a half percent of the construction costs of state projects. While no law sets limits in New York State, in the past the governor or agency head responsible has appointed an ad hoc commission to select works of art for a new undertaking. During construction of the Albany Mall in the seventies, Governor Nelson Rockefeller of New York appointed a committee of advisers to acquire art for the state's Executive Department, and the legislature appointed its own committee to select works for its quarters. Between 1965, when Robert F. Wagner was mayor, and 1983, New York City budgeted monies for art in its public-works projects. Architects for the projects recommended acquisitions, which required approval by the New York City Fine Arts Commission, composed of representatives from cultural institutions and other appointees of the mayor. A percent-for-art program was passed by the New York City Council in 1983. Similar programs exist in other major cities of the United States and Canada, including Atlanta, Chicago, Los Angeles, Miami, Philadelphia, St. Louis, San Francisco, Seattle, and Toronto. The Federal Government, under the aegis of the General Services Administration, permits the use of a half percent of construction costs for the purchase of art, with selections proposed by panels named by the National Endowment for the Arts.

In recent years, private corporations, including most of the Fortune 500, have also placed works of art in both public and private areas of new headquarters and office buildings. Among corporate patrons in the New York-New Jersey Metropolitan Region are the Chase Manhattan Bank, American Telephone and Telegraph, Public Service Electric and Gas Company, Citicorp, Prudential Insurance Company, and Philip Morris Incorporated.

The Port Authority takes advantage of outside resources in making acquisitions of art. The United States Department of Transportation funds programs for the placement of art in transportation facilities. The Anthony Padovano sculpture *Spherical Division*, 1975 (page 91), at the Journal Square Transportation Center, Jersey City, New Jersey, was acquired with funds provided by the Department of Transportation under a demonstration grant to revitalize the city. Art in Public Places, sponsored by the National Endowment for the Arts, in part underwrote Ilya Bolotowsky's mural *Marine Abstraction*, 1979 (page 90), for the New York City Passenger Ship Terminal and the conservation of Arshile Gorky's 1936–37 Newark Airport murals (pages 58, 59).

A public art program can be approached in at least four ways. First, public agencies can stimulate the procurement of art by providing incentives for the developer, who then makes the selections independently. A second approach is to let the architect play the leading role, proposing works of art to a commission or panel with no other power than to reject or approve his or her selections. A third approach is to set up an ad hoc panel, usually composed of art experts and/or artists, which is dissolved once work is selected for a single project. The fourth approach is a continuing and a participatory one. Here the architect, lay officials, and art experts work together on the selection of art.

The Port Authority's approach is participatory. Through its Committee on Art, the architect, public officials, and art experts all come together to review each project, recommend modes of art and the procedure for selecting it, and finally choose the art itself.

The Port Authority Committee on Art is com-

Right:
Joan Mondale, Honorary Chairperson, Federal Council on the Arts and Humanities, with artists James Biederman, left, and Ilya Bolotowsky, center, at dedication of Bolotowsky's *Marine Abstraction*, New York City Passenger Ship Terminal, and of Biederman wall painting, World Trade Center, 1979

Below:
Port Authority Executive Director Peter C. Goldmark, Jr., Henry Geldzahler, former New York City Commissioner of Cultural Affairs, and James Brooks at rededication of artist's WPA mural *Flight*, Marine Air Terminal, La Guardia Airport, 1980

Top: Model for south
wing waiting room, Port
Authority Bus Terminal
renovation, 1978

Artist George Segal,
right, supervising
installation in 1982 of
The Commuters, 1980, in
completed bus terminal

posed of:
1. two members of the Port Authority Board of Commissioners,
2. the Executive Director,
3. the Chief Architect,
4. the architect for the project under consideration, and
5. outside consultants knowledgeable in the arts.

The members of the first Committee on Art, set up in 1969 by the Honorable James C. Kellogg III, then Chairman of the Board, were Commissioners Hoyt Ammidon and W. Paul Stillman; Mrs. Charles W. Engelhard, trustee of The Metropolitan Museum of Art, New York, and The Newark Museum and later to become a Port Authority commissioner; Executive Director Austin J. Tobin; Chief Architect Gordon Lorimer; World Trade Center architect Minoru Yamasaki; and Dorothy C. Miller, Senior Curator Emeritus of Painting and Sculpture, The Museum of Modern Art, New York. Gordon Smith, Director of the Albright-Knox Art Gallery, Buffalo, joined the committee during its first year.

The committee's first major project was the World Trade Center, whose designer, Yamasaki, had specific spaces for art in mind. He called for three sculptures in the plaza, a sculpture for the West Street entrance, a wall tapestry for Two World Trade Center, and a sculpture for the interior lobby of One World Trade Center, both facing the plaza. Yamasaki had already selected two of the three plaza sculptures. After considering the work of over fifty prominent artists, the committee recommended New York sculptor James Rosati for the third plaza sculpture and suggested a stabile by Alexander Calder for the West Street entrance (Calder proposed a sculpture 150 feet high, and Yamasaki proposed scaling it down to 14 feet; they finally agreed on 25 feet). The com-

mittee wanted Spanish artist Joan Miró to create the tapestry and the New York artist Louise Nevelson to make the lobby sculpture. Although both artists agreed, their works were long in coming to fruition. Miró's wall hanging was acquired in 1977, Nevelson's assemblage in 1978.

The committee drew on its experience with the World Trade Center to establish procedures for the selection of art for other locations. Initially, the architect makes a saturation study showing all possible areas where art might be placed in a newly proposed project. Then he provides a master plan stating his preferences in terms of space, mode, and, in some cases, artist. The committee reviews his recommendations before making its suggestions of artists and forms. Once the master plan is approved on a large-scale project, the committee determines the final selection procedure.

As an example of this process, we can trace the steps by which George Segal's *The Commuters*, 1980 (pages 86–87), came to be placed in the south wing waiting room of the Port Authority Bus Terminal. In 1975, the commissioners authorized the renovation of the terminal, calling for the addition of a new wing and the rehabilitation of the existing space. The project architect, Roger Carroll of the Port Authority, was asked to do the two studies for the inclusion of art. He developed the saturation and master plans for the project, submitting them for evaluation and approval by the Committee on Art. The master plan called for five works of art, three on the walls and two freestanding, with suggested sites and recommendations on the types of art and materials desired.

The committee then decided on the process to follow in selecting art for each site. For the waiting room sculpture, the committee established an invitational competition. An outside nominating committee suggested artists to be invited to com-

José de Rivera,
Flight, 1938,
Collection The Newark
Museum, on extended
loan to Newark Interna-
tional Airport, 1974–77.
Work commissioned 1936
by WPA for Newark Air-
port but never installed.

sion; Doris C. Freedman, president of both the Municipal Art Society of New York and the Public Art Fund; Isabel Fernandez, Executive Director of the New York Creative Artist Project; and Barbara Furst, Chairman of the New Jersey State Council on the Arts. Also participating were the expert members of the Committee on Art: Dorothy C. Miller; Samuel C. Miller, Director of The Newark Museum; and Thomas M. Messer, Director of The Solomon R. Guggenheim Museum, New York. Members of the nominating committee worked independently, unrestricted in their choices by consideration of the artists' nationalities, where they worked and lived, or their reputations.

The nominators submitted more than a hundred names. Some artists, among them George Segal, appeared on more than one list. Letters of invitation were then sent to all artists recommended. Those interested in entering the competition were given its rules as well as the physical characteristics of the space under consideration. They received blueprints, renderings of the waiting room from various perspectives, technical data on load-bearing limitations, and safety and fire-code requirements. Each artist met with a representative of the Port Authority and was encouraged to visit the site and observe the varying traffic patterns around it.

Although the competition had been conceived as invitational, the committee decided to open it to any artist interested. Over two hundred and fifty artists responded and one hundred and twenty-two submitted proposals. The competition rules required the artist to submit a photograph, slide, or model. These photographs, slides, and models were then submitted to the consulting curator, Dorothy Miller, for her review. Miss Miller narrowed the choice to twelve entries. The full committee was shown all the submissions and added only five works to Miss Miller's

pete. The Chairman of the Port Authority Board of Commissioners appointed participants to the committee: Romare Bearden, distinguished artist and member of the New York State Council on the Arts; Barbaralee Diamonstein, art critic and member of the New York City Fine Arts Commis-

list. At a subsequent meeting the committee selected five finalists: Pol Bury, Linda Howard, Clement Meadmore, George Segal, and Chris Wilmarth. Each of the five was given the opportunity to meet with the Port Authority staff to review with them in detail the materials to be incorporated in the work, its fabrication, proposed siting, technical specifications with regard to site, and maintenance requirements. The artists were given freedom at this point to make any additions or changes they pleased. Nearly all submitted changes or supplemental material. Each was committed to a definite price for the work. The refined proposals were then submitted to the full Committee on Art.

The committee selected George Segal's entry as the winner. This recommendation was submitted to the Board of Commissioners and following their approval, accepted by the governors of both New Jersey and New York. The process of selection, begun in December 1978, was completed nearly one year later, in November 1979.

A different process was followed in the selection of works of art for Kennedy International Airport. Here the committee decided to favor the region's emerging artists, visiting galleries and studios, viewing fifteen hundred submissions by artists, dealers, museum curators, and art consultants. Some five hundred works were submitted for final selection by the full committee, and over two hundred works from this group were eventually selected to form the basis of the collection.

The Port Authority also plays a role in organizing temporary exhibitions. At nearly all its public facilities, the Port Authority has cooperated with community and art groups in sponsoring changing art events. Exhibitions have featured works by Helen Frankenthaler, Robert Irwin (page 54), José de Rivera, and Richard Serra (page 52). Other artists whose work has been on exhibi-

tion are Alice Adams, Bill Barrett, Stanley Boxer, Jeffrey Owen Brosk, John Chamberlain, John Cross, Mel Edwards, Kosso Eloul, Harriet Feigenbaum, Francis Hines, Joel Janowitz, Lila Katzen, Bridget Kennedy, Betty Klavun, Phyllis Mark, Salvatore Romano, Alan Sonfist, Jason Strawn, Julius Tobias, Norman Tuck, Alexandre Wakhevitch, and James Wines. These exhibitions have been jointly sponsored by the Port Authority and institutions such as The Metropolitan Museum of Art, The Newark Museum, and the Whitney Museum of American Art and organizations such as the Lower Manhattan Cultural Council and the Public Art Fund.

In addition, works from the Port Authority collection have been lent for exhibitions across the United States to such institutions as the Art Institute of Chicago; the Dallas Museum of Fine Arts; the Everson Museum, Syracuse, New York; The Solomon R. Guggenheim Museum, New York; the High Museum of Art, Atlanta; the Hirshhorn Museum and Sculpture Garden, Smithsonian Institution, Washington, D.C.; the Houston Museum of Contemporary Art; the Los Angeles County Museum; the Queens Museum, New York; and the Walker Art Center, Minneapolis. An exhibition of great significance to the Port Authority was organized by Ruth Bowman for The Newark Museum in 1978. Entitled "Murals without Walls: Arshile Gorky's Aviation Murals Rediscovered," it grew out of the rediscovery of two panels from the Gorky Newark Airport mural cycle, *Aviation: Evolution of Forms under Aerodynamic Limitations*, 1936–37 (pages 58, 59) commissioned by the Federal Art Project of the Works Progress Administration (WPA) in 1936. The murals had been painted over in the forties by the military when it took control of the airport. The discovery of the two panels was a joint effort on the part of Ruth Bowman, Dorothy Miller, and

Committee on Art
reviews proposed
acquisitions. Saul
Wenegrat, standing;
seated, Thomas M.
Messer, Director, The
Solomon R. Guggenheim
Museum; Dorothy C.
Miller, Senior Curator
Emeritus, The Museum
of Modern Art, New York;
and Samuel C. Miller,
Director, The Newark
Museum. Back to camera,
Alan Sagner, Chairman,
Board of Commissioners

Guy Tozzoli, Director,
World Trade Depart-
ment, Austin J. Tobin, Ex-
ecutive Director, the Port
Authority, and Harold
Gleason, President,
Franklin National Bank,
examine model of World
Trade Center, 1969

The Port Authority.* Samuel Miller, Director of The Newark Museum and a member of the Committee on Art, invited Ms. Bowman to organize the exhibition to dramatize the plight of these murals and other WPA artworks that had met a similar fate. The Newark Museum, with the assistance of the National Endowment for the Humanities, presented "Murals without Walls." This exhibition, together with a film produced for public television, appeared in major cities throughout the United States. The two panels are now on extended loan to The Newark Museum.

One of the Port Authority's most rewarding joint undertakings involved the CETA Artists Project. Funded by the U.S. Department of Labor through the New York City Department of Employment, the project was administered by the Cultural Council Foundation. Heading the program was Rochelle Slovin, assisted in the visual arts by Suzanne Randolph and Joseph Giordano. A number of spaces on Port Authority property where art had not been included were made available to the CETA artists. Most of these projects involved murals in public places: Cynthia Mailman's *Commuter Landscape*, 1979 (page 111), in the World Trade Center PATH Station; Alan Samalin's *Picturing Flight*, 1982 (page 66), at Kennedy International Airport's Control Tower; and wall paintings by Hunt Slonem, Germaine Keller (page 104), and James Biederman at the World Trade Center. CETA artists were also employed in a major attempt to improve the Ninth Street PATH Station in Manhattan. Using the station's empty advertising display space, artists Akira, Ellsworth Ausby, Bimal Banerjee, Robert Carvin, Herman Cherry, Stanford Golob, John Gruen, Francine Halvorsen,

*Although Ruth Bowman, Dorothy Miller, and I had begun the search for the murals, it was Steve Stempler of my staff who made the actual discovery. He found some threads at the edge of a wall and brought them to my attention. Larry Majewski, a conservator from New York University, confirmed the finding.

Germaine Keller, Wyn Loving, Kurt McGill, and Kwok-Yee Tai organized *Rock Paper Scissors*, 1978, for which they created original prints.

No endeavor of this magnitude can take place without the support and good will of a great many people. A debt of gratitude is owed first to Austin J. Tobin, Daniel Kurshan, and Harvey Sherman, without whose enthusiasm and working contributions the Port Authority art program would not have begun. The collection would not have been possible without the genius of two great women, Dorothy Miller and Jane Engelhard, who have remained with the Committee on Art since its inception. Members of the Port Authority staff who have made valued contributions include Maria Aasland, the late Roger Carroll, Alexander Demaras, Paula Fanning, Gordon Lorimer, and Sheldon Wander. Others within the Port Authority who have been enthusiastic supporters of the program include Robert Aaronson, Sidney Frigand, Louis Gambaccini, Gene Gill, Frank Gorman, Neal Montanus, Victor Strom, Anthony Tozzoli, Guy Tozzoli, and Joseph Vanacore; also Susan Baer, Robert Kelly, Donald Burns, "Ike" Dornfeld, Ronnie Eldridge, Jack Gartner, Walter Giordano, William Munroe, George Peirce, Mario Salzano, Lloyd Schwalb, and Stephen Stempler. This catalog would not have been possible without the help of Karen Sexton, Registrar, assisted by Grace Campbell, Fran Morin, Bertha Puchal, and Madeline Schroth. Finally, acknowledgment must be made of the integrity, standards, and devotion of the Committee on Art, Jane Engelhard, Dorothy Miller, Samuel Miller, Thomas Messer, Chairman Alan Sagner, Vice Chairman Mayor Robert F. Wagner, and Executive Director Peter C. Goldmark, Jr., as well as the past members of the Committee, without whom the program could not have been carried on.

Art
for the Public

James Rosati
Ideogram. 1974
Stainless steel,
23' 6" x 19' 6" x 28' 6"
Commissioned 1969;
completed and installed
1974. World Trade Center
(Austin J. Tobin Plaza)

Ceremony celebrating opening to public of Joan Miró's *World Trade Center Tapestry* in 1976. From left, Gérard Gaussen, French Consul General; Mrs. Charles W. Engelhard, Commissioner and member of Committee on Art; Louis de Guiringaud, French Ambassador to the United Nations; Minoru Yamasaki, World Trade Center architect; and Thomas M. Messer, Dorothy C. Miller, and Samuel C. Miller, members of Committee on Art

The Art Collection: Its Formation

DOROTHY C. MILLER
Senior Curator Emeritus
of Painting and Sculpture
The Museum of Modern Art,
New York

It was in June of 1969 that Austin J. Tobin, then Executive Director of the Port Authority of New York and New Jersey and the man who in many ways extended the character and range of the organization, asked me to become a member of the art committee that was being appointed to select works of art for purchase for the World Trade Center, still in construction.

Mr. Tobin suggested that I join him, Mrs. Charles W. Engelhard, distinguished art collector and later to become one of the Port Authority's commissioners, and Commissioner Hoyt Ammidon for a day's trip to Detroit to confer with Minoru Yamasaki, architect of the World Trade Center, at his headquarters. We studied the architect's master model of the center, with its two towers and other buildings surrounding the five-acre plaza. The focus of our meeting that day, and of many meetings to come, was the choice of works of art for the plaza and for the enormous lobby walls of the two towers.

The first commission had already been given several years earlier by the architect himself to Fritz Koenig, well-known German sculptor, to design the fountain that dominates the center of the plaza (pages 92–93). He had also started negotiations with the noted Japanese sculptor Masayuki Nagare, who had submitted a model for a black-granite sculpture for the Church Street entrance to the plaza. The Committee on Art studied Nagare's model and voted in favor of commissioning him to produce the sculpture. It was completed in 1972 and installed in 1974 (page 99).

At its first meeting in October 1969, the Committee on Art agreed at once that the collection must represent outstanding American artists and those of other nations. Alexander Calder and Louise Nevelson were cited at this meeting and a stabile by Calder was commissioned later in 1969 for the World Trade Center.

Calder, born in Philadelphia in 1898, was the son and grandson of sculptors. His grandfather, Alexander Milne Calder, made the figure of William Penn for Philadelphia's City Hall. His father, Alexander Stirling Calder, made one of the two figures of George Washington flanking the great arch at the north entrance to Washington Square, New York. His *Washington in Peace*, 1918, balanced the figure *Washington in War* done in 1916 by Herman A. MacNeil.

Graduated in 1919 as a mechanical engineer from Stevens Institute of Technology, Hoboken, New Jersey, Calder soon turned toward art and studied at the Art Students League, New York. Long sojourns in Paris, where he first exhibited wood and wire sculptures in 1927, alternated with living in New York and Connecticut. In Paris he made his animated *Circus* (Whitney Museum of American Art, New York) and numerous wire sculptures, such as *Josephine Baker* (The Museum of Modern Art, New York). From them evolved his famous "mobiles," abstract sculptures with moving parts, first shown in Paris, and then in New York, in 1932. Initially miniature in scale but later monumental in proportions, Calder's mobiles, imitated but never equaled, remain his unique and extraordinary contribution to modern art. Long before the Committee on Art came into existence, the Port Authority collection already contained a major mobile sculpture by Calder, *Flight*, 1957 (frontispiece), installed in the Main Hall of the International Arrivals Building at John F. Kennedy International Airport, at the suggestion of Skidmore, Owings & Merrill's Gordon Bunshaft, the architect who designed the building.

For some years before his death in 1976, Calder had been spending much of his time in France, working in his country studio near Saché. The fields surrounding his studio were filled with the wonderful objects that would later find homes in urban settings around the world. These were his "stabiles," sculptures that have many parts but do not move. When in 1969 the Committee on Art commissioned a stabile for the World Trade Center, it based its selection on an existing sculpture, *Three Wings* (see pages 28–29), in black painted steel, now in the Louisiana Museum, Humlebaek, Denmark. Under Calder's direction, a new version of *Three Wings* was made, enlarged to a height of twenty-five feet and painted red. This piece Calder named *World Trade Center Stabile*, 1971 (page 32), although with typical whimsy, he thought it should be called "The Cockeyed Propeller."

The lobbies of the two towers at the World Trade Center each have an immense white marble wall, one hundred feet wide and fifty feet high, visible from the plaza through the outer glass walls. The Committee on Art in 1970 decided to ask two world-renowned artists to accept commissions for works for these two walls. They were Spain's great modern master Joan Miró and the famed American sculptor Louise Nevelson.

Early in 1970, the committee wrote to Miró about producing a wall hanging thirty-five feet wide for the lobby of Two World Trade Center. Born in Spain in 1893, Miró was well-acquainted with the United States, having made many visits here. His work is to be found in major museums, universities, public buildings, and private collections. Highly skilled in the innumerable techniques of modern art, including some of his own invention, Miró, who died in 1983, was one of the unquestioned giants of twentieth-century art. Shortly before his correspondence with the Port Authority, Miró had developed, with the artisans in the workshop of Josep Royo in Barcelona, his *sobreteixims*, which James Johnson Sweeney later described as "fringed rugs with heavily knotted surfaces or specially woven, rough jute mats with bold splashes of paint and free-swinging hiero-glyphs, to which have been affixed skeins of colored wool, heavy loosely coiled rope, scored or numbered scraps of canvas." His small wool "collages" set the stage for his major effort to come.

On hearing from the Port Authority, Miró sent word from his home in Palma de Majorca that he was interested in a work of the great size required. He asked that he might collaborate with his weavers at the Royo workshop. The Committee on Art, unable to comprehend Miró's extraordinary new technique from his description and the inadequate photographs he was able to provide, hesitated to make a definite commitment for a work of such size and cost. However, Miró, with irrepressible enthusiasm, went ahead without having received a definite commission and produced an immense work, intending it for New York. It was shown at the Grand Palais in Paris in the great Miró retrospective of 1974; two members of the Committee on Art saw it there and heartily recommended it. The great work was therefore sent to New York on approval and hung in Two World Trade Center in 1976.

On the occasion of the unveiling of his great wall hanging, Miró, who took great pleasure in the collaborative process, wrote to the committee describing the "adventure" of the collaboration and the "risks" he and the artisans had taken together. Popularly and critically well-received in New York, the Miró was bought in 1977 and promptly dubbed the *World Trade Center Tapestry* (page 7). The Port Authority is indeed fortunate in having not only an exemplary work by this extraordinary artist, but also one then technically unique.

The work of art hanging on the lobby wall of One World Trade Center is, like the Miró, a unique invention of the artist's imagination. Louise Nevelson's immense sculptured relief, *Sky Gate, New York* (page 95), was made in 1977–78 and was

Louise Nevelson assembling *Sky Gate, New York* in lobby of One World Trade Center, 1978

installed in 1978. Seventeen by thirty-two feet, the great sculpture was assembled in Nevelson's famous manner from innumerable pieces of wood, small and large, and painted black, to form a great organized unit in a medium completely original and truly inimitable.

Louise Nevelson was born in Kiev, Russia, in 1900, and has lived in America since early childhood, when the family went to Rockland, Maine. She moved to Manhattan around 1920 and has lived there ever since, with frequent trips all over the world in connection with her many sculpture exhibitions and with commissions for her work, which have been eagerly sought by museums, government institutions, and private art collectors, worldwide, since the early forties.

These two immense works of art, the Miró and the Nevelson, can be seen from the plaza of the World Trade Center, and are overwhelming in their impact when one stands directly beneath

them. They provide an unusual experience for the visitor. Nothing on this scale, by two such famous modern artists, can be found together in one place in New York.

Another project undertaken by the Port Authority that has brought satisfaction to the American art world has been the unexpected recovery of "lost" mural paintings by artists working from 1935 to 1943 on the Federal Art Project. In 1934, in the depths of the Depression, President Franklin D. Roosevelt established the Works Progress Administration, under the direction of Harry L. Hopkins, to "save the skills of American workers," thousands of whom had no jobs. Artists and craftsmen were not forgotten, and the Works Progress Administration (later named the Work Projects Administration) included the Federal Art Project, of which Holger Cahill was national director throughout its eight years of existence. By the end of 1935, that is, in less than half a year, the Art

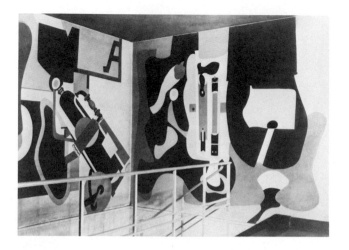

Left: Installation view, **Arshile Gorky,** *Aviation: Evolution of Forms under Aerodynamic Limitations,* 1936–37, Newark Airport. Photograph dated April 17, 1940

Right: Mayor Fiorello H. LaGuardia and Gorky at opening of WPA Federal Art Project Gallery, New York, 1935. On wall, study for lost panel of Newark Airport mural

Project had employed three thousand, seven hundred and ninety-five artists on three hundred and twelve projects throughout the United States. For the first time in American history, a great number of artists were given the opportunity to design and carry out mural paintings, mosaics, and monumental sculptures on the walls of public buildings.

These murals and sculptures, like all works of art produced by the Federal Art Project, were allocated to tax-supported institutions: schools, colleges, hospitals, government buildings, and so on. In spite of the fact that these works of art were the property of the United States Government, many of the mural paintings were in later years painted over and thus obliterated, or actually ripped off the walls and destroyed. Easel paintings, small sculptures, and prints disappeared through negligence and theft. Many murals done under government auspices by talented young artists, then little known but later to become famous, have been sought in vain, but determined efforts to find traces of them are continuing.

A great stimulus toward this rediscovery of lost mural paintings was given by the Port Authority of New York and New Jersey when it brought to light murals done by two distinguished American painters, Arshile Gorky and James Brooks. The rediscovered paintings by

Gorky were two of ten panels painted in 1936–37 under the Federal Art Project for the second floor of the administration building of the recently built Newark Airport (pages 38–39). The Gorky panels had been painted over, and some were possibly torn off the walls, when the United States Army took over Newark Airport in 1941 during the war. The two surviving panels are called *Aerial Map* and *Mechanics of Flying* (pages 58, 59).

Gorky, an American born in Turkish Armenia in 1904, came to the United States in 1920, living first in Providence and Boston, then moving to New York about 1925. Like so many others, he was living in extreme poverty during the Depression, despite achieving some recognition soon after arriving in New York. He studied and taught at the Grand Central School of Art, and in 1930, accepted an invitation from Alfred Barr to exhibit three paintings at The Museum of Modern Art in "46 Painters and Sculptors under 35 Years of Age." In the autumn of 1935, along with his friends Stuart Davis and Willem de Kooning, Gorky joined the Federal Art Project. A year later he began painting the Newark Airport murals, *Aviation: Evolution of Forms under Aerodynamic Limitations.* Before his employment by the Federal Art Project, he was briefly enrolled in an earlier United States Government program, the

Public Works of Art Project administered by the Treasury Department, for which he began to design a mural he called "1934" for the "Port Authority Building." This was probably the Port Authority's 1933 building on Eighth Avenue between Fifteenth and Sixteenth Streets. Had Gorky not been dropped from the project in 1934, the Port Authority might have owned another mural by this later-acclaimed painter.

In the summer of 1940, James Brooks, also employed on the Federal Art Project, began work on the mural painting *Flight* (pages 60–61) for the huge circular space of the Marine Air Terminal at LaGuardia Airport. Brooks recalled years later that he had been influenced in his thinking, as had so many artists throughout the world, by Picasso's great masterpiece *Guernica*, 1937, which was shown in Alfred Barr's 1939 Picasso exhibition at The Museum of Modern Art and which remained in New York at the Museum, on loan from the artist, for some forty years thereafter. Possibly the great size of the *Guernica* as well as its tremendous expressive power lent encouragement to Brooks, the young muralist who was setting out to cover a canvas two hundred and thirty-five feet long. For the next two and a half years Brooks would be painting the LaGuardia mural, working from models, from Leonardo's notebooks of early flying devices, and from contemporary books on flight (pages 42–43). He was using a new medium developed by the Technical Division of the Federal Art Project, a synthetic resin and casein emulsion, which achieved a matte surface along with a resistance to atmospheric conditions prevailing close to the ocean.

Brooks, born in 1906, had come to New York from Texas. His path had crossed Gorky's at the Grand Central School of Art, which he entered in 1927, later studying at the Art Students League. Brooks, like many others for whom the Federal Art Project had made mural painting possible for the first time, was keenly aware of the reputation of the Mexican mural painters and their actual presence in New York. In 1931 José Clemente Orozco had painted murals in the New School for Social Research. In 1933 Diego Rivera was invited by Rockefeller Center to paint a mural seventeen feet high by sixty-three feet long in the tallest building, that of the Radio Corporation of America. Brooks remembers that he was one of the many New York artists who observed the famous Mexican muralist at work, painting night and day on a high scaffold in full view of the public. In the late summer of 1933, Brooks corresponded with Rivera, asking for and receiving permission to watch the Mexican at work on murals for the New Workers School on West Fourteenth Street. Rivera's Rockefeller Center mural was left unfinished and then painted over in 1934. Although Brooks's mural was also painted over (just when is unclear), it was successfully rescued by the Port Authority in 1980.

A mural by another outstanding American artist, Ilya Bolotowsky, was commissioned by the Port Authority in 1977 and dedicated in 1979 at the New York City Passenger Ship Terminal on the Hudson River. Forty feet wide by four feet high, the ceramic tile mural *Marine Abstraction* (page 90), mounted above the information desk of Terminal C, is visible from the entrance to the pier. Born in St. Petersburg, Russia, in 1907, Bolotowsky came with his parents to the United States in 1923, becoming an American citizen in 1929. He taught and exhibited in New York and elsewhere, and is represented in leading American museum collections. He died in a tragic accident in 1981.

Another important American sculpture commissioned by the Port Authority stands in a place through which many thousands of people who

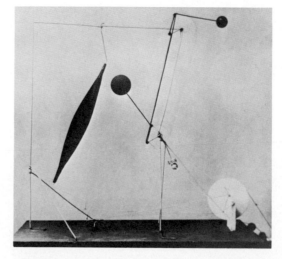

Alexander Calder
"The Motorized Mobile That Duchamp Liked."
c. 1932
Duchamp named Calder's motor-driven constructions "mobiles" and arranged their first showing at the Galerie Vignon, Paris, 1932

Below: Calder installs mobile *Flight*, 1957, at Kennedy International Airport

Opposite:
Three Wings, model for *World Trade Center Stabile*, in foreground; Calder's studio, Saché, France, 1960s.

Installation view,
Nicholas Krushenick,
The Iron Butterfly, 1968,
International Arrivals
Building, Kennedy
International Airport

live in New Jersey and work in New York pass daily. This is the south wing waiting room of the Port Authority Bus Terminal in New York. The artist, George Segal, born in 1924 and living in New Jersey, won an invitational competition for this sculpture, *The Commuters* (pages 86–87), commissioned in 1980 and installed in 1982. Segal has said that his sculpture reflects his own thirty years of experience commuting from South Brunswick, New Jersey, to New York City: "I feel strongly that public art should concern itself with what means a great deal to people who pass by."

As we have seen, most of the major works of art acquired by the Port Authority of New York and New Jersey have been commissioned. The two sculptures by Alexander Calder are outstanding examples. *Flight*, of 1957, in the International Arrivals Building at Kennedy Airport was probably the earliest commission. The second sculpture by Calder, the *World Trade Center Stabile*, was also a commission, this time recommended by the Committee on Art. The stainless-steel sculpture by James Rosati at the World Trade Center was chosen in 1969 by the Port Authority from a group of perfectly rendered small models, all made since 1962; the models signalled a radical change of style from Rosati's carving and modelling to a Constructivist mode in which he renounced volume and mass as sculptural elements. Rosati's *Ideogram* (page 21), the piece chosen by the Committee on Art, was enlarged to monumental size and installed in the plaza of the World Trade Center in 1974 under the supervision of the artist and the architect, the location having been decided upon by the Committee on Art.

Other commissioned work includes the mural decorations for the Port Authority Bus Terminal, New York, by J. Esteban Perez, *Constructivist Space Drawing* (pages 88–89), 1981, and by Yaacov Agam, *Reflection and Depth*, 1984.

The Port Authority also acquired the works of young or obscure artists of quality. Its great commissions for prominent locations necessarily went to major painters and sculptors. One occasion arose, however, when a large number of works by artists of less than towering fame could legitimately be bought. This was in 1970–71 when Gordon Bunshaft's International Arrivals Building at Kennedy International Airport was expanded to accommodate the increasing number of travelers flying into the airport. Long corridors leading from the waiting rooms to the airplanes and other parts of the airport seemed to beg for something to look at. Therefore, more than two hundred paintings, sculptures, drawings, and prints by some fifty artists were purchased to give color and interest to those long corridors and to provide visitors with a preview, however brief, of some of the unfamiliar and innovative work of America's artist population.

The World Trade Center offered the Port Authority of New York and New Jersey its first opportunity to assemble a number of great works of art in a single location. From its initial plan to its present realization, the fine arts program of the Port Authority has set a splendid example for the inclusion of the arts in a great public building program. In the thirties, New York's Rockefeller Center performed a similar function, incorporating painting and sculpture in the design of its complex of buildings. However, in the half century since the building of Rockefeller Center, knowledge and acceptance of contemporary art have grown so tremendously that the Port Authority has been able to include in its art collection some of the most advanced art of our time, a goal not readily attainable in the earlier period.

Alexander Calder
World Trade Center
Stabile. 1971
Red painted steel, 25′
high
World Trade Center
(Corner of Church and
Vesey Streets)

The Public Agency as Patron

SAM HUNTER
Professor
Department of Art
and Archaeology
Princeton University

The Port Authority's historical relationship to the visual arts began in the thirties with its completion of the George Washington Bridge, one of the most dramatic and one of the largest suspension bridges in the world. When the Port Authority later leased the facilities of the Newark and LaGuardia airports, a cultural bridge was thereby built to the imaginative Federal art programs that proliferated under President Franklin D. Roosevelt, for the airports contained extremely significant Works Progress Administration (WPA) mural cycles by Arshile Gorky and James Brooks, respectively. The murals were well-known, but no longer visible. They had, in fact, disappeared in the intervening years under layers of paint applied by zealous but misguided officials with no clear awareness that they were committing artistic vandalism. Part of the Gorky cycle vanished altogether, but once the remaining murals' locations were definitely reestablished during the seventies, the Port Authority undertook the herculean task of uncovering them, layer by fragile layer of overpaint. They have now been successfully restored, and are publicly accessible once again. The extant Gorky murals are on long-term loan to The Newark Museum in New Jersey, and the James Brooks painting presides in situ, as originally installed, on the walls of LaGuardia's Marine Air Terminal.

The Port Authority made its first independent gesture of support for placing art in a public space in 1957. Alexander Calder was commissioned to construct a monumental mobile forty-five feet in its widest extension for the new International Arrivals Building of the New York International Airport (later renamed for John F. Kennedy)[1] at Idlewild, Queens. For the next decade little more transpired, but by the late sixties a renascence of public art was under way, bearing unexpected fruit when the Port Authority began construction of its ambitious World Trade Center. A number of elements conspired to make it plausible and even advisable for the Port Authority to commission monumental sculptures for the five-acre plaza of the building site. Some background in the historical development of American public art, and of large-scale sculpture particularly, is necessary to appreciate the surprising new turn of events.

Sustained by the creation in 1967 of the Art in Public Places program by the National Endowment for the Arts (NEA), encouraging public art through matching grants to public and private institutions and community groups, and by the new flow of corporate largesse with the formation in that year of the Business Committee for the Arts under David Rockefeller's leadership, monumental sculpture began to bloom on outdoor sites in the late sixties with surprising frequency. To set the stage, there were such pioneering ventures as Doris C. Freedman's exhibition "Sculpture in Environment," twenty-six three-dimensional works dramatically placed in New York's urban outdoor spaces in 1967, under the sponsorship of the city's Department of Recreation and Cultural Affairs. That same year the first postwar monumental sculpture of significance designed for a highly visible public space made its debut in Chicago, when Picasso's *Head of a Woman* (page 35), enlarged from the artist's maquette, was erected in the Civic Center.[2]

Henry Geldzahler, former Commissioner of New York City's Department of Cultural Affairs and Director of the Visual Arts Program of the National Endowment for the Arts from 1966 to 1969, deserves a share of the credit for providing the impetus for the proliferation of large-scale sculptures in outdoor urban sites. The process began in earnest when he persuaded the people of Grand Rapids, Michigan, to match Washington's outlay of $45,000, under its new Art in Public

Places program, for the purchase of an enormous red Calder stabile. *La Grand Vitesse* (page 36) was commissioned in 1967 and installed in 1969 in an urban renewal area, even though objections were registered to its presence. Today the Calder sculpture is generally recognized as the first and archetypal American public sculpture of heroic scale subsidized by government in the postwar era. It has, incidentally, revolutionized Grand Rapids' aesthetic outlook, spurring further commissions for a number of other fine public sculptures, and given the city a new sense of pride and civic identity. The Calder silhouette is now the municipal logo and appears on everything from official stationery to city garbage trucks (page 36).

The virtual explosion of public sculpture, whose ubiquity today leaves us all somewhat blasé, was not simply a product of unprecedented opportunity in the realm of patronage but depended on new techniques for fabricating large-scale sculpture ingeniously developed in workshops such as Lippincott of North Haven, Connecticut. The popularity in the sixties of the Minimalist style, with its geometric simplicity, archi-

Tony Smith
Moses. 1975
Black painted steel,
11′ x 15′ x 84″
Seattle Center, Seattle,
Washington. Commissioned by Seattle City
Light 1% for Art Fund,
National Endowment for
the Arts, Contemporary
Art Council of the Seattle
Art Museum, and
Virginia Wright Fund,
Courtesy Seattle Arts
Commission

tectural ambition, and strong industrial presence, also encouraged the rebirth of the monumental-sculpture genre. Heroic sculpture on outdoor sites had become a dominant feature of art by the seventies, and perhaps even a permanent cultural legacy. The last great flowering of public sculpture on a comparable scale dates back to the declining phase of Beaux Arts monumentalism before World War I, when neo-Roman and Baroque statuary flooded the landscape with what art historian Milton W. Brown aptly termed "an orgy of plastic commemoration."[3] After the war those pompous, dated allegories of great deeds and national heroes, immortalized in imperishable stone and bronze, slipped into senescence, a casualty of changing times and the revolution in artistic taste.

For nearly half a century, between the activities of Augustus Saint-Gaudens (1848–1907), Beaux Arts practitioner, and Tony Smith (1912–1981), the acknowledged pioneer of large-scale Minimalist sculpture on outdoor sites in America, monuments were out of favor. The tradition of public art had revived briefly with the noble but abortive experiment of the WPA Federal Art Program from 1935 to 1943, although mural painting was very much the ascendant form at the time. For the most part, neither the social occasion, sustained patronage, nor the artistic impulse existed for making large-scale, three-dimensional art, nor for venturing beyond the studio environment during the period between the wars in the United States.

Today, however, public sculpture, and, indeed, public art in other mediums, is a familiar and accepted phenomenon. Following the dominant artistic trend of our time, public art is mainly abstract, oblique in content and meaning, and on occasion environmentally challenging either in scale or in the use of site and natural materials. Although public sculpture in particular often stirs popular rancor, at least when it first appears, it has for the most part won wide community acceptance and finds a permanent home all across the nation at countless urban and suburban sites, in shopping malls and industrial parks, on Federal, state, and municipal plazas. The public-art phenomenon began to gather momentum in the mid-sixties, shortly after the death in 1965 of David Smith, whose late Cubi series prophesied the popularity of abstract sculpture in architecture scale by Tony Smith, Robert Morris, Ronald Bladen, Mark di Suvero, and others shortly thereafter. The immoderate size of the Abstract Expressionist canvases of Barnett Newman and Jackson Pollock were also factors in the emergence of large-scale sculpture, which defied indoor gallery and museum spaces and seemed destined only for outdoor display.

In the seventies the triumph of the new public art was firmly secured. Almost any new corporate or municipal plaza worthy of its name deployed an obligatory large-scale sculpture, usually in a severely geometric, Minimalist style; or where more conservative tastes prevailed and funds were more generous, one might find instead a recumbent figure in bronze by Henry Moore or one of Jacques Lipchitz's mythological creatures. Today there is scarcely an American city of significant size boasting an urban-renewal program that lacks one or more large, readily identifiable modern sculptures to relieve the familiar stark vistas of concrete, steel, and glass.

The forces that created the favorable atmosphere for public art in the sixties had a direct impact on the development of the Port Authority art program. With the construction of the World Trade Center, the architect Minoru Yamasaki sought and received the approval of his client in 1968 to commission Fritz Koenig's monumental

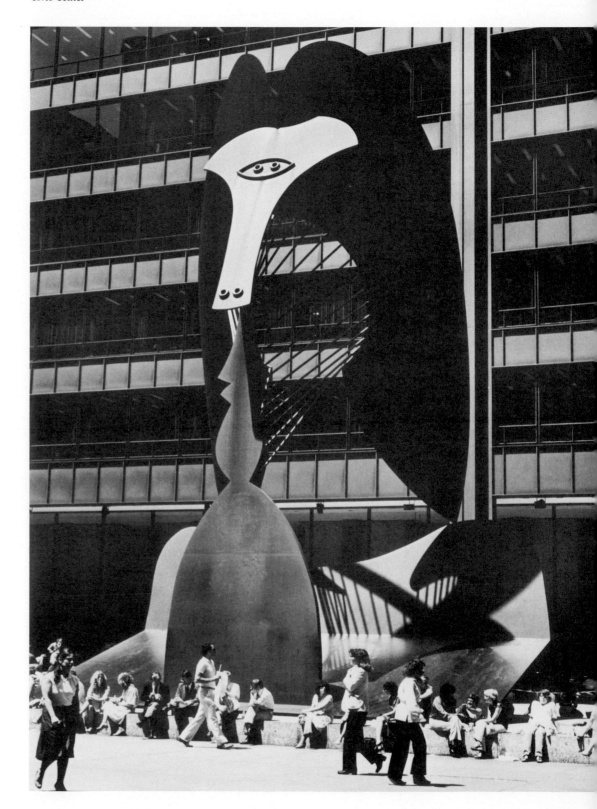

Alexander Calder
La Grande Vitesse. 1969
Red painted steel,
43' high
Vandenberg Center Plaza,
Grand Rapids, Michigan
Commissioned by city of
Grand Rapids with the
aid of a grant from the
National Endowment for
the Arts.

Below: Grand Rapids
sanitation truck with
logo of *Grande Vitesse*

fountain as the centerpiece of the Austin J. Tobin Plaza at the World Trade Center. The large and complex sculpture was installed in 1972.

Saul Wenegrat of the Port Authority has noted the conditions that led to the formation by the Port Authority of a systematic art program:

> Around us was a growing awareness of the place of public art. Nelson Rockefeller was then Governor of New York, and he was very interested in seeing that all the agencies in the state supported art. Given this impetus, and the fact that the architect, Yamasaki, wanted art in his large plaza—after all, it was five acres, three times the size of St. Mark's—we agreed to install some large sculptures there.[4]

Although the commissioners were pleased with the fountain maquette, they also came to the realization that a thoughtful and complex art acquisition program, involving sizable expenditures of public funds, required expert advisers on familiar terms with the professional art world and recent directions in art. The recommendations of these advisers in an area as controversial as contemporary art would give the final selection authority, and could be argued from various perspectives, based both on pragmatic experience and on clearly rationalized general principles.

To assist the Port Authority Board of Commissioners in the selection process, therefore, the officials of the bistate agency established the Committee on Art. The subsequent choices of plaza sculpture, the important tapestry of Joan Miró for the lobby of Tower Two, and Louise Nevelson's grand wall relief for the lobby of Tower One were made by the Committee on Art, which was officially constituted in 1969.[5]

Today, in every new building or renovation devised by the Port Authority, one percent of capital construction costs is set aside for art purchases. This percent-for-art program compares favorably with the dispensations for new buildings at Federal, state, and municipal levels,[6] and it may be unique among independent state agencies. Thus, the Port Authority, much like other more visible and exalted government bodies, finds itself engaged in the important cultural task of giving meaning to the process of upgrading the urban environment and expanding the definition of public art. It is a challenging communal dialogue that has generated considerable controversy in recent years.

Although the generous flow of current art expenditures may conceivably run dry one day, should new construction finally come to a halt, there is little likelihood that the completion of the Port Authority art program is at hand. Building projects currently on the drawing board and those already underway, such as additions to Newark International Airport, assure a continuing round of art acquisitions for many years to come. In the meantime, the Port Authority has managed to acquire a varied group of works, ranging from monumental sculptures in stone and metal such as those that adorn the plaza of the World Trade Center to the modest works on paper hanging in airport lobbies, offices, and other public areas. More than three hundred and fifty artists are represented.

The Port Authority currently has six major facilities where acquisition programs are active or where significant historical works have been rediscovered and made publicly accessible. In the chronological order of their execution, the recovered works are, first, Arshile Gorky's two surviving murals from a cycle of ten completed in 1937 and known by the arcane and ponderous title *Aviation: Evolution of Forms under Aerodynamic Limitations* (pages 58, 59). They were painted for the old Newark Airport Administration Building under the auspices of the WPA. James Brooks's mural, *Flight*, 1940–42 (pages 60–61), also WPA-sponsored, was resurrected from its shroud of blue overpainting in 1980, and can now be seen in the rotunda of LaGuardia Airport's Marine Air Terminal. At the International Arrivals Building of John F. Kennedy International Airport hangs the 1957 Calder *Flight* (frontispiece), his first truly monumental mobile designed for a specific indoor space. The departure lounges, corridors, and other public spaces of the building have been filled with a generous selection of contemporary paintings, tapestries, prints, and a smaller group of sculptures (pages 64–85) as part of a continuing acquisitions program begun in 1969. One of the patronage roles the Port Authority envisages for itself is the encouragement of new and emerging talents by the purchase and display of their work

Below left: Newark
International Airport
Administration Building,
in 1975, where two panels
from Arshile Gorky's
WPA mural cycle were re-
discovered in 1972

Right: Gorky at work in
1936 on *Activities on the
Field*, panel intended for
north wall of
Administration Build-
ing's second floor

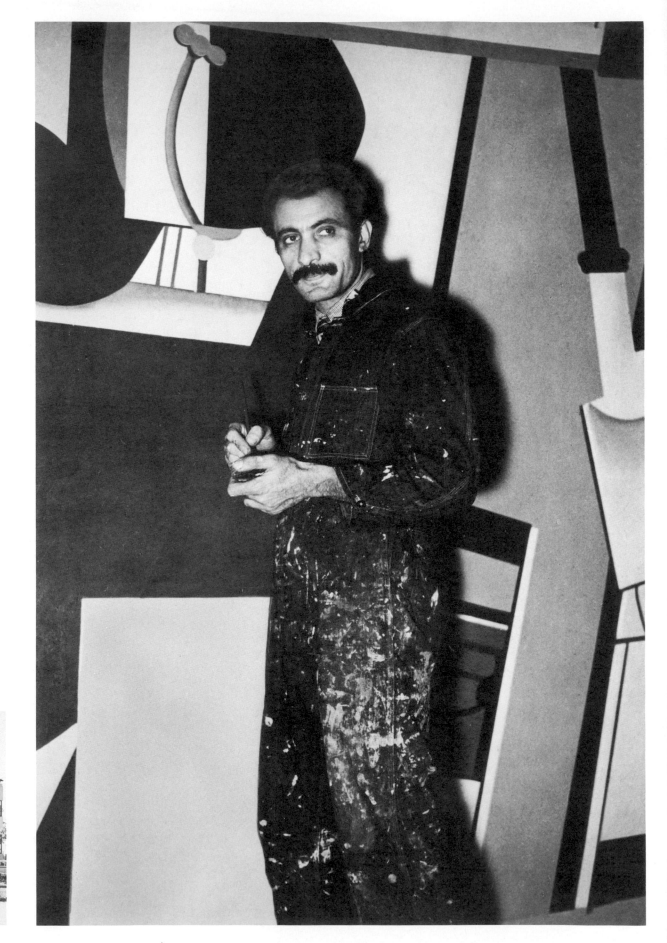

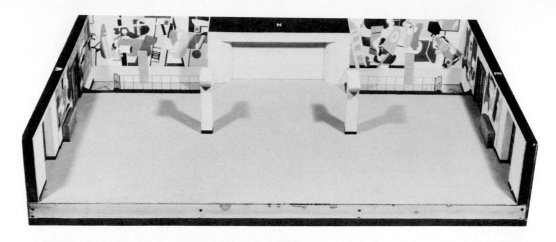

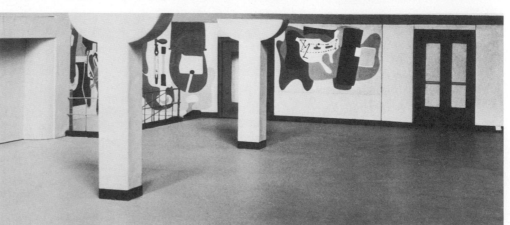

Model of Arshile Gorky's *Aviation: Evolution of Forms under Aerodynamic Limitations* created for exhibition "New Horizons in American Art," The Museum of Modern Art, New York, in 1936. Photographs of model are only surviving evidence of entire cycle of ten panels. Top, view from south; second, south wall containing four panels of Modern Aviation series (at extreme left, study for surviving panel *Mechanics of Flying*); third, west wall containing two panels in Early Aviation series; bottom, east wall containing studies for surviving panels *Mechanics of Flying*, at left over staircase, and *Aerial Map*, at right. See color plates (pages 58, 59)

before they have attained wide recognition.

The most ambitious integrated art program was created for the World Trade Center; it is also the most valuable Port Authority property, with its construction costs yielding a generous budget for major art commissions. On the plaza and adjoining it are these monumental sculptures: Calder's *World Trade Center Stabile*, completed in 1971 and installed in 1974 (page 32); Fritz Koenig's *Sphere for Plaza Fountain*, cast in 1971 and installed in 1972 (page 93); Masayuki Nagare's *World Trade Center Plaza Sculpture*, completed in 1972 and installed in 1974 (page 99); and James Rosati's *Ideogram*, 1974 (page 21). In the lobby of Tower One hangs Nevelson's *Sky Gate, New York*, completed in 1978 (page 95), and in Tower Two, Miró's monumental tapestry of 1974 (page 7), installed in 1976.

In 1979 the late Ilya Bolotowsky installed the ceramic mural *Marine Abstraction* (page 90) in Terminal C of the New York City Passenger Ship Terminal, built by the Port Authority for the City of New York and designed by Eliot Noyes to accommodate ocean travelers. *Marine Abstraction* was acquired through the aid of a matching grant from the National Endowment for the Arts' Art in Public Places program. Bolotowsky had been a distinguished muralist in an abstractionist mode of painting since the Depression, when he was active in the WPA Federal Art Project. As a founding member of the influential American Abstract Artists organization in 1936, he joined such figures as Stuart Davis, Arshile Gorky, Willem de Kooning, George L. K. Morris, and others in propagating an aesthetic position that was sufficiently open-ended and flexible to encompass a wide range of abstract styles, including geometric elements and biomorphic forms. The avant-garde association contributed significantly to the later flowering of American Abstract Expressionism in

the forties. Bolotowsky's rigorously geometricized Passenger Ship Terminal mural expands and refines the rationalist style he had begun to explore with notable success in the thirties.

The final important location is the dramatically renovated Port Authority Bus Terminal, which acquired early in 1982 George Segal's figure group in bronze with white patina, *The Commuters*, 1980 (pages 86–87). Unlike the acquisitions for the Trade Center, this sculpture was selected after an invitational competition that drew more than one hundred proposals.

The Gorky murals are almost as appealing for the mystery of their rediscovery and the diligent restoration that brought them to light as they are for their intrinsic artistic merit and historical interest. The murals had disappeared and were long ago presumed destroyed. They were rediscovered in 1972 by a Port Authority employee who found a telltale thread of canvas obtruding from a hole in an area where the murals' presence had only been suspected. As early as 1970, Dorothy C. Miller, long familiar with these abstract works by one of the most valued of the WPA-supported artists, suggested to a fellow member of the Committee on Art that the Port Authority search for the lost murals, but their actual discovery was the direct result of the indefatigable efforts and genteel badgering of art historian Ruth Bowman, then Curator of the New York University Art Collection. She refused to believe the entire cycle had been swallowed up, although previous investigations had yielded no trace of them. She engaged the Port Authority in the search that led to their dramatic rediscovery. After removing a tiny fragment from the wall showing the canvas thread, expert restorers found one of the murals intact under fourteen layers of house paint. A further search led to the discovery of a second panel. Removed from the wall to a restoration studio in

Boston, the murals were systematically relieved of the coats of paint that had inexplicably been applied by the Army Air Corps during World War II.

Originally, the bold, abstract mural cycle covered more than fifteen hundred square feet of wall space with a rhythmic sequence of tensely interlocked, brilliant-hued color planes, which commented as eloquently on the artist's facile assimilation of Fernand Léger and Miró as on modern theories of flight. Only two of the ten large wall panels were recovered and restored.[7] *Aerial Map* (page 58) is a fanciful and ingenuously lopsided map of the United States in flat, brightly colored abstract shapes; Gorky once explained that this part of the cycle was concerned with "the wonder of the sky."[8] A second strongly patterned and more formally diverse canvas presents a recognizable cross-section of cylindrical devices to record wind speed, direction, and barometric pressure. It is appropriately called *Mechanics of Flying* (page 59).

Much like certain phases of abstract and environmental art today, Gorky's murals in their own time stirred heated debate and controversy. Dorothy Miller, then a young curator at The Museum of Modern Art, New York, had included Gorky's model and one completed panel in an end-of-first-year survey of WPA art, "New Horizons in American Art," opening in September 1936 at the museum (pages 38–39). The murals were greeted with abuse by the press, and the WPA forwarded a request for a written opinion of them to the museum's director, Alfred H. Barr, Jr. Defending Gorky's contemporary relevance, Barr argued ingeniously for the modern spirit:

> Any conservative or banal or reactionary decorations would be extremely inappropriate. It is dangerous to ride in an old-fashioned airplane. It is inappropriate to wait and buy one's ticket surrounded by old-fashioned murals. One of the greatest mysteries of modern life is the enthusiasm for streamlined trains, automobiles and airplanes shown by people who at the same time are timid when confronted by equally modern painting.[9]

Gorky died tragically by his own hand in 1948 at the age of forty-four, in a state of despondency occasioned by serious reversals in his personal life and health, and dismayed by a fire that had consumed the contents of his Connecticut studio. Like Pollock, he became a legendary figure in American art soon after his demise, although only in the past few years has his work received the serious study and scholarly scrutiny it merits. The Newark Airport murals undoubtedly constitute the most ambitious project of his early maturity, carried out at a time when his concepts of art were still in transition. The paintings are clearly extrovert and public rather than intimate or diaristic, and they lack the quality of personal anguish of his later, more introspective works. Still, the surviving canvases from the airport walls must be regarded as irreplaceable evidence of an emerging major talent. They mark an important transition in American art from a derivative and predictable purist geometry to the more personal expressionist abstraction that dominated the postwar era.

In 1980 the Port Authority unveiled and rededicated James Brooks's mural *Flight* (pages 60–61) at the LaGuardia Airport's Marine Air Terminal, a handsome Art Deco building. The two-hundred-and-thirty-five-foot decoration for the rotunda is one of the most ambitious murals commissioned by the WPA (in this case, by the New York City WPA Art Project).[10] It had been painted out for some twenty-five years, however. Unlike the Gorky mural, which had been partly destroyed, *Flight* had been simply covered over with

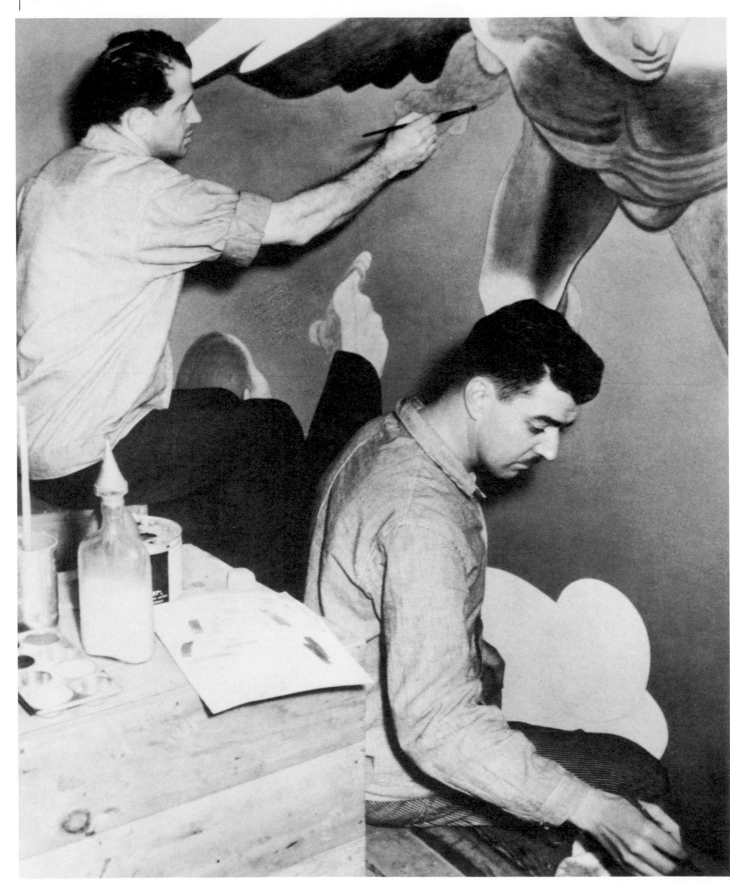

James Brooks, lower right, with assistant Ben Katz at work in August 1940 on first panel of *Flight* for Marine Air Terminal, LaGuardia Airport

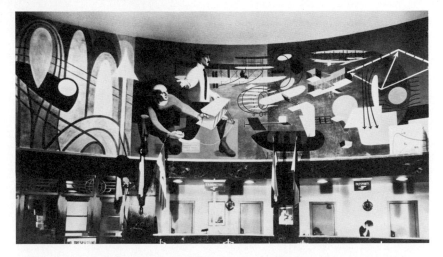

Marine Air Terminal, LaGuardia Airport: top, in 1975; second, at completion of the Brooks mural *Flight* in 1942; third, in 1975, after mural had been painted over; bottom, during restoration of mural in 1980

paint by the Port Authority when it took over the airport from New York City in the mid-fifties. Today Brooks believes the popular press castigated his painting on imaginary political grounds in the hysterical atmosphere of the McCarthy period, and that the purely abstract nonallusive forms in his wall painting were mistakenly fantasied as Communist symbols concealing such images as the hammer and sickle. Abstract art itself was commonly viewed with suspicion at the time. There is even a recorded incident where Brooks was comically accused of leftist sympathies because the majority of his figures seemed left-handed to one observer. This was reported by Barry Newman in the *Wall Street Journal* in an article whose headline also suggests the kinds of depredations that overtook so many worthy public projects of the WPA art program: "That Fabulous Airport of Flying-Boat Days is Yecch-Blue Now."[11]

In its own time the mural was acclaimed, however. Edward Alden Jewell, senior art critic for *The New York Times*, devoted a full page of his Sunday art section to it. Jewell described the epic project as "a sound and well-sustained and sincere performance…one of the most satisfactory murals, on so vast a scale, thus far produced by an American artist."[12]

Flight is divided into three main sections that represent the history of man's aeronautical aspirations. Figures of myth, history, and fantasy are combined with purely abstract imagery in the first section, which Brooks called "Imagined Flight." It represents man's attachment to the earth, as well as the legendary flight of Daedalus and his son Icarus, the latter depicted as falling after his wax wings were melted by the sun.

In the middle section, "Release," and in the third, "Flight Accomplished," Brooks depicts man's attempt to build his own wings and escape from the earth, recapitulating Leonardo da Vinci's flying devices, Wilbur and Orville Wright's first powered flight at Kitty Hawk, North Carolina, in 1903, and, finally, the popular Pan American Clipper flying boat then in use at LaGuardia Field, as the airport was then known.

The artist's own explanation of *Flight* at the time it was completed probably best captures the mural's iconographic meaning:

> The design is not intended to reproduce literally episodes from the history of man's conquest of the air, but to recreate the wonder that was and is still felt at the phenomenon of man's leaving the earth and soaring through the air. It utilizes not historical events but historical attitudes toward flying. The single aim of the design is to identify the spectator…with the broad scope of man's yearning for flight and its final realization.[13]

On a formal level, the large painting presents itself as both a commanding architectonic design and a skillful exercise in lyrical abstraction. Picasso's great canvas *Guernica*, 1937, and Miró's biomorphic fantasies in paintings such as *The Hunter (Catalan Landscape)*, 1923–24, which similarly shuttle between imagery and a fluent abstraction, were both acknowledged influences. Brooks's fantasy of abstract colored shapes representing Leonardo's aerodynamic experiences is painted in bright, flat lozenges of green and a virulent red-orange, color combinations that prophesy the artist's chromatic invention in his purely abstract painting of the late forties and subsequent decades. His rather blunt, Giottoesque figuration and refined abstract decoration play off one another in the brilliant mural, resulting in a typically controlled yet vital creative resolution.

The fourteen-month restoration of the mural

was carried out by conservator Alan Farancz, with one-half the restoration cost paid for by the Port Authority and the other half funded equally by Laurance S. Rockefeller and the late DeWitt Wallace, founder and by then retired publisher of *The Reader's Digest* (page 46). The Port Authority had sought funds to defray restoration expenses, and after failing to arouse interest in the art world enlisted the help of an aviation magazine to mount an exhibition dramatizing the plight of the Brooks murals, which tests had proven existed in sound condition beneath the many layers of paint. Both major donors were "aviation buffs," and they also had a long history of philanthropic support of the arts. Since this was not a percent-for-art project, the Port Authority turned to the private sector for financial help.

Beginning in 1969 the Committee on Art made a concerted effort to find art in a variety of mediums, ranging from mural-scale wall paintings to print portfolios, to adorn and embellish the walls of the newly enlarged International Arrivals Building of Kennedy International Airport. More than two hundred works have been selected and installed in the extensive facility over the intervening years. They are hung in the second-floor spaces adjoining the large entrance hall where the monumental and extremely handsome Calder mobile imperiously reigns, gently moving on otherwise imperceptible air currents amid the inert flags of all nations. Upstairs, the East and West Wings, the "fingers," or corridors, that radiate from them to the individual departure lounges, and the lounges themselves are hung with works in diverse mediums and styles. There are a number of large tapestries woven from the designs of Jean Arp (page 64), Sonia Delaunay (page 76), Miró, and Picasso (page 72); paintings by such minor masters as Bolotowsky (pages 65, 74); and paintings, prints, and sculptures by the emerging talent of the early seventies, including Victoria Barr, John Button, Janet Fish, Hans Hokanson, Nicholas Krushenick, Alvin Loving, Harvey Quaytman, Gabrielle Roos, and John Salt.

In the West Wing hang four monumental tapestries by Calder in his characteristic vivid primaries with dynamic wriggling black shapes

Left:
Joan Miró
The Hunter (Catalan Landscape). 1923–24
Oil on canvas,
25½" x 39½"
The Museum of Modern Art, New York

Right:
James Brooks
Detail of *Flight*. 1940–42
Marine Air Terminal
LaGuardia Airport

and geometric signs (*Many Triangles*, page 78) animating the public spaces outside the Alitalia, Swissair, and SAS lounges. These agitated forms make an instructive contrast to the rippling light reflections of Willy Weber's highly polished stainless-steel relief construction, *Space Dream*, 1971, whose active surfaces match the optical energies of Calder's tapestry configurations. In the East Wing Loving's shaped canvas, *Diana: Time Trip, II*, 1971 (page 68), is also optically active, with its patterned surface and twisting rectangles recalling the unresolvable intricacies of a Rubik's Cube in two-dimensional projection. Hokanson's carved construction *Helixikos, No. 18A*, 1971 (page 57), provokes a response that hovers between an intellectual savoring of its geometric form and an unrestrained pleasure in the sensuous quality of its rough-hewn natural wood. The international flavor of the lounges is upheld by works such as the elegantly precise and decorative construction in tautly wrapped yellow canvas, *Construction No. 28*, 1970, by the Ecuadorian, Luis Molinari-Flores, and the lithograph *La Mascara*, 1969 (page

83), from a series of an expressionist, fantastic character by the Mexican painter José Luis Cuevas.

The group of four paintings by Janet Fish of magnified and meticulously realistic commonplace objects, among them *Two Boxes of Lemons*, 1970, and *Vinegar Bottles*, 1972 (page 71), and John Salt's familiar iconography of a derelict car interior in *Skylark*, 1969 (page 77), recall different aspects, hard and soft, of the contemporary Photo-Realist tendency, which registers the world of fact without comment or *parti pris*, emulating the model of the camera lens. The curious psychological neutrality and impassivity of Photo-Realism contrast dramatically with the careless rendering, visual dynamics, and animalistic imagery of Karel Appel's silkscreen series of half-human creatures, given such evocative titles as *Looking to the Infinite* and *Walking Alone*.

In the East Wing, Gabrielle Roos's sequence of five large, horizontally oriented abstractions present soft color fields, stained and tinted into the canvas weave, divided and reintegrated by

Artist James Brooks, second from right, points to detail of his restored WPA mural *Flight* at rededication in 1980. From left, Alan Sagner, Chairman, Board of Commissioners; Laurance S. Rockefeller, patron of the restoration; Mrs. Fiorello H. LaGuardia, widow of the Mayor; and Alan Farancz, the mural's restorer

bleeding vertical bands of more assertive color, as in *No. 13*, 1971 (page 79). Her color fields continue and expand upon the rigorous structural refinements of Bolotowsky's admirable model, as in *Pale Yellow and Blue Tondo*, 1970 (page 74), rooted in thirties abstraction and a more doctrinaire aesthetic theory. They also prepare us for the blunt shock, heroics of scale, and simplistic design of Jerry Okimoto's untitled shaped canvas of 1970 (page 70), with its color brilliance and cleanly delineated edges. Harvey Quaytman's hybrid painting/object, *Moon Fancy*, 1969 (page 70), raises questions about the physical as well as the perceptual character of contemporary painting by discreetly separating a wedge of canvas from its support.

A tour of the lively collection in the International Arrivals Building is very much like the experience of circulating through a comprehensive, intelligently selected contemporary museum survey of the art of the seventies. The works on view exhibit and articulate most of the influential styles that made history in that decade, from the latter-day followers of Abstract Expressionism to Pop art and varieties of realism.

The sculptures for the World Trade Center Austin J. Tobin Plaza and the hangings for the interior tower spaces together represent the most comprehensive and architecturally integrated art program to date in a Port Authority facility. Fritz Koenig's twenty-five-foot-high bronze sphere (page 93) was commissioned to form the central element in a black-marble fountain with a basin ninety feet in diameter. The symbolism of the sphere, which also rotates imperceptibly, is not explicit. However, it does seem to bear a distinct relationship to Italian sculptor Arnaldo Pomodoro's monumental burnished spheres in bronze, objects whose breaks, ruptures, and internal complexities evoke images of a flawed perfection and technological entropy. Philosophically and metaphorically, the cleft spheres by both sculptors evoke images with humanist and existential implications in the postwar world, offsetting their common source in the purity and innocent idealism of Brancusi's pristine geometries.

The second commission recommended by the architect and approved by the newly constituted art committee in 1969 was an immense sculpture in black granite with a low-lying, horizontal configuration of a double pyramid, made by the Japanese sculptor Masayuki Nagare (page 99). Reputed to be the largest public work in stone in existence, barring Mount Rushmore, the sculpture has an estimated weight of three hundred tons. Mounted on a marble and granite base, the black-granite sculpture is thirty-four feet long, seventeen feet wide, and fourteen feet high. The design consists of two asymmetrical lobes, polished to high brilliance and separated by a rough gulley resembling a dry, rocky streambed. Despite its insistent horizontality and gently sloping peaks, which threaten to lose scale against the overwhelming verticality of the two super skyscrapers of the World Trade Center and adjoining buildings, the ensemble effectively holds its own, creating a strong and offsetting presence. It is reminiscent of the monumental, isolated stones set in a bed of raked sand in the famous Ryūanji Garden in Kyoto, similarly evoking a mood of Eastern reticence and meditation. Such stylized conventions have a meaningful symbolism for Nagare, who seriously studied Zen Buddhism and Shintoism as a young man.

Calder's 1971 sculpture for the World Trade Center (page 32), is one of his finest large freestanding constructions of a type known as the stabile. The eminently logical rubric was coined by Jean Arp to distinguish these static sculptures rooted to terra firma from the sculptor's motorized and wind-activated kinetic forms, suspended on intricate armatures, that Marcel Duchamp had called mobiles (page 29). In the early thirties Calder began to make stabiles, and as time went on he conceived them on a progressively more monumental scale until he made one that reached the height of sixty feet, *Teodelapio*, created for the outdoor sculpture exhibition at Spoleto in 1962 and ultimately acquired and permanently installed by the Italian city. The *World Trade Center Stabile* was made at the Etablissements Biémont, a foundry Calder patronized in Tours, France, near his French home and studio at Saché, where he more or less permanently settled in 1963. Calder had made a fourteen-foot-high maquette, *Three Wings* (page 28), at Biémont and then supervised its enlargement to twenty-five feet in heavy gauge steel in 1970-71. Like many of the Minimalist constructions of the sixties and seventies by his younger colleagues, Calder's magnificent stabiles became increasingly monumental and environmental in their expansive powers at the end of his life.

The enlarged, swelling Miróesque shapes, sizzling orange-red color, and emphasis on welding seams and rivets in the *World Trade Center Stabile* contribute to an intensified material and formal presence. Although Calder used biomorphic and/or geometric shapes on a vast scale, he managed to achieve a contradictory lyrical presence and an anti-gravitational lightness through the refinement and chromatic intensity of his playful forms. Calder insisted that his sculpture be kept out of the World Trade Center plaza, and in accordance with his wishes it was set up on the sidewalk, thus functioning less as an aloof "monument" than as an animating catalyst for the surrounding life of an active street corner.[14]

The subtly angled geometric volumes and controlled tensions of James Rosati's stark steel sculpture *Ideogram*, 1974 (page 21), both echo and defy the polished, rippling aluminum skin and ambiguities of light reflection and scale of the twin skyscrapers and hotel that stand beside it. Unlike the buildings, which are, in a sense, all flat surface to be taken in from one vantage point, Rosati's skewed form can only be appreciated fully when viewed from every angle. The large scale and ponderous sense of weight are destabilized by the cantilevered, angled crossbeams in highly polished stainless steel. The subtly tilted, bulky volumes are reminiscent of David Smith's late Cubi series. They appear from certain angles to defy gravity and create a rather precarious balance of metal beams that seem in danger of toppling but manage to achieve a satisfying stability after all.

Installed in the mezzanine lobby of One World Trade Center, Louise Nevelson's large, black-painted wood relief, *Sky Gate, New York*, 1977–78 (page 95), measuring seventeen by thirty-two feet, is one of her largest and most effective "walls," made up of a fascinating assortment of found and shaped newel posts, finials, parts of balustrades, chair slats, and barrel staves. The individual histories or identities of the myriad components vanish in a unified totality. Nevertheless, even this rigorously stylized work, a collection of treasured trophies with their associations muted and preserved in a fresh formal synthesis of Constructivist character, retains a slightly fantastic air. Despite its abstract rigors, the intricate and labyrinthine assemblage conveys a sense of poetic mystery rather than one of clarity and precision usually associated with the Constructivist genre.

At the dedication ceremony Mrs. Nevelson described her sculpture as "a night piece," which represents the "windows of New York." She said she had looked at New York's skyline and translated its silhouette in her sculpture. And of its setting she said:

> The World Trade Center is two giant cubes and the tallest building in the city. The towers stand there among the rest of the sculpture-city and they are fine. They're magnificent. When the lights go on at night they're touching beyond the heavens. But when you think of the concept of building involved in the World Trade Center, it has set a precedent and challenge to the world that the human mind has encompassed the engineering of that space.[15]

Mrs. Nevelson likes to point out that she has in recent years undertaken three major commissions in the City of New York. In addition to the wall relief for the World Trade Center, there are the elaborate multiform reliefs and freestanding structures in wood for the Chapel of the Good Shepherd at St. Peter's Lutheran Church, in the midtown Citicorp building, and her downtown sculpture park on the triangular plot bounded by Maiden Lane and Liberty and William streets now known as Louise Nevelson Plaza, which has an impressive array of seven monumental sculptures (page 51).

"They are all of a piece. They could be in one room," she insists.[16] Where others might see a refreshing variety, she finds only continuity and integration in her three New York sculpture commissions. All these works bind her even more closely to the city that has strongly marked and identified her artistic development for nearly sixty years, and which constantly refreshes her spirit as she still reconnoiters the streets near her SoHo studio, collecting her familiar "found" sculpture elements of castoff wood.

The Miró tapestry (page 7) that hangs in the mezzanine lobby of the south tower represents the art committee's most dramatic coup. It was the artist's first monumental tapestry designed for a public space in this country, thus anticipating a later work of comparable scale commissioned for the new East Building of the National Gallery of Art in Washington, D.C., by several years. It also reflects a particularly creative experimental moment in Miró's *oeuvre*. He had never considered the medium until his daughter fell victim to a tragic accident that almost cost her life. He rewarded the hospital staff that saved her by acceding to their request for a large-scale tapestry. Shortly thereafter the Port Authority art committee approached Miró with their own proposal of a large hanging. After consulting with his friend Alexander Calder, Miró felt reassured and decided he, too, would enjoy the exposure to a fluid mass audience in a busy public space. He proceeded to make the tapestry for the marble walls of the mezzanine lobby. He completed the massive, three-ton hanging in time for his great retrospective exhibition at the Grand Palais in Paris in 1974. It was placed on exhibition at the World Trade Center two years later and acquired in 1977.

The tapestry is Miró's first monumental weaving to approximate a series of powerfully expressive smaller wall hangings crafted in the workshop of Josep Royo, Barcelona, in the late sixties; those hangings had less to do with conventional flat tapestries than with the rope collages Miró fashioned in the twenties and early thirties. The rough woven grounds, rope strands, and thick pile of the World Trade Center hanging are, indeed, strongly reminiscent of Miró's abrasive Dada/Surrealist collages, even though the imagery is more pacific and the jarring surface eruptions have been smoothed away into a harmonious textural unity.

The vibrant primary and intermediate colors

and the intense black calligraphy of Miró's paintings of the early seventies are recapitulated in the weaving with a startling vividness. Even the effect of charcoal markings and the mottled grounds of his paintings is brilliantly simulated. Miró's atmospheric color space is also evoked with a startling verisimilitude in this magnificent collaboration between the greatest living artist of our time and a remarkably skillful craftsman in tune with his sensibility. Royo succeeds in using conventional fibers and wool, normally found in flat tapestries, in a new manner to create a composition that is three-dimensional and conveys the sense of a sculpted relief. In terms of quality, ambition, and expressive force, the hanging must rank with the finest of Miró's myriad collaborative and reproductive works in graphics and ceramics, and with his rare pieces of monumental sculpture in bronze.

In April 1982 the Port Authority dedicated George Segal's *The Commuters*, 1980 (pages 86–87), a group of three life-size figures in white bronze shown standing on line before an entrance gate at the Port Authority Bus Terminal, New York, waiting to board a bus. This is the first major artwork for the terminal renovation, begun in 1975.

For Segal, who lives in nearby New Brunswick, New Jersey, and frequently commutes by bus from there to New York, the commission seemed natural, even inevitable, despite the lively invitational competition. "The Port Authority terminal is forever in my mind," he had said some time before the project materialized. "A lot of my mental life has been spent there."[17] Although the site readily suggested the theme of the work, the location assigned him in the terminal tested the sculptor's ingenuity. The sculpture had to be placed in a circular area of open floor space (page 14), surrounded by ticket windows and benches, and intensely illuminated from above by a circle of bright lights—"I have never used so many lights in my life," Segal commented.

Resolved to harmonize his work with "all the arbitrary, man-made, man-designed moves in the space," he created a sparc tableau of three white bronze figures (simulating his more familiar body impressions cast from life in plaster for which he is best known). They are an assortment of typical habitués of the terminal (actually modeled from his wife, Helen, and a New Brunswick couple, the sculptor George Kuehn and his wife Carol). Arranged on a diagonal axis in a file across the waiting room area, the figures convey an insistently horizontal movement that projects the paths of their arrested progress. The surroundings of the terminal, now refurbished and starkly modernistic, provide an authentically alienating environment for these ghostly commuters, locked forever in the same motion as their hastening viewers who occasionally mistake them for the real thing.

Working in a style of genre realism but with ambiguous currents of both romantic sentiment and an irony allied to Pop art, Segal has become one of our most popular and effective public sculptors. His long list of successfully achieved commissions is impressive. In the context of the Port Authority's discriminating patronage and its commitment to finding art of quality for its heavily populated public spaces, Segal's comments on the public art issue are of particular interest and relevance. He has said of himself and his colleagues who find themselves "riding the new wave of public art" somewhat uneasily:

> We all came from an elitist background. Artists used to belong to a private club, essentially. Now the question is whether you can maintain your eliteness, the density of your subject matter, a decently high level of thinking, and still be ac-

cessible to a lot of people.[18]

Despite his occasional nagging doubts, Segal is convinced that we are experiencing a genuine moment of cultural change, one of those rare periods when art and life become mutually sustaining, and the artist should join it rather than stand aloof. He says: "Something rings true about it. People are hungry for some common belief. Everyone wants to feel attached to something larger than himself."[19]

In its adventurous exhibition program, the Port Authority has entered into a new kind of partnership with other government agencies, community groups, and nonprofit organizations, making available to them and to individual artists some of its space for the display of more radical works of art that challenge popular conceptions about public art. In successive years it played host to the Avant-Garde Festival, first at the World Trade Center in 1979 and then at the Passenger Ship Terminal in 1980. The Port Authority has also combined its efforts with the Cultural Council Foundation's CETA Artists Project in funding special works, including *Rock Paper Scissors*, 1979–80, designed for temporary installation in the Ninth Street PATH Station, New York; and four murals in long-term installation at the World Trade Center: three on the forty-third floor (Germaine Keller, *PATH Mural*, 1979, page 104) and one in the World Trade Center PATH Station (Cynthia Mailman, *Commuter Landscape*, 1979, page 111).

The Port Authority has offered other institutions and individual artists exhibition room at its various facilities. In the course of an average year, four loan shows are generated from such sources as the Lower Manhattan Cultural Council and the Public Art Fund, Inc. The projects of these progressive, nonprofit groups are invariably on the cutting edge of current avant-garde productions.

Louise Nevelson
Shadows and Flags. 1978
Seven Cor-Ten steel
sculptures
Louise Nevelson Plaza,
New York

In 1981, for example, Francis Hines stretched a monumental cat's cradle of nylon parachute cloth between and around the brick columns of the new Port Authority Bus Terminal in a complex design that consciously emulated the steel trussing on the exterior facade. In 1983 he created another fabric construction (page 54), this one celebrating the twenty-fifth anniversary of the Kennedy International Arrivals Building, where his work occupied the Main Hall. Hines is known for his wrapping of New York's Washington Square Arch, completely encasing the lower Manhattan monument in nylon fabric.

A more discreet, indeed, virtually imperceptible, project in which the Port Authority cooper-

Richard Serra
Arc. 1980
Cor-Ten steel,
12′ x 200′ x 2 ½″
St. John's Rotary,
New York
Installed by The Port
Authority of New York
and New Jersey, the
Public Art Fund, and Leo
Castelli Gallery

ated was Robert Irwin's *Line Rectangle*, 1977 (page 54), which stretched a fabric cord between the rooftops of two symmetrical office buildings in the World Trade Center plaza, forming an elegant aerial rectangle. The public installation, an environmental extension of Irwin's concurrent one-man show at the Whitney Museum of American Art, New York, demonstrated the artist's concept of art as the projection of ideas that must make themselves known beyond the museum context.

Perhaps the most challenging exhibition for which the Port Authority contracted was the installation of Richard Serra's *Arc*, a curving twelve-foot-high two-hundred-foot-long steel wall erected in 1980 at St. John's Rotary, a raked white-gravel island formed by the roads leading from the Holland Tunnel on the New York side. With its austere, mustard-colored Cor-Ten surface unrelieved by detail or formal incident giving it a derelict industrial look, the immense spread of steel presents a perceptual and intellectual challenge. When Serra created a tilted wall of comparable scale and brute surface in another context, invading the architectural and human environment of a Manhattan Federal Building plaza, a great hue and cry was set up both in the press and among employees working in the building. The St. John's Rotary *Arc* suffered no such fate, perhaps owing to its relative isolation from pedestrian traffic and the more concentrated activities of daily life: the sculpture is experienced almost exclusively through the window of a car when passing by. It will occupy its current site at least through 1986, when The Museum of Modern Art will mount a retrospective exhibition.

Like Serra's other brutally powerful constructions, the work is designed to be experienced intellectually as well as physically. The artist also conceives it as an exercise in perception for a viewer in locomotion, who becomes increasingly attentive to the long arc's perimeters as they slide in and out of view. The unusual location of the work represents a new Port Authority initiative of installing interesting works at various entry points to the city. For Serra, on the other hand, *Arc* embodies multiple ambiguities, which he expects will assure the work a persisting problematic character despite its simple form and engage the viewer, whether vehicular or pedestrian, in an adversary relationship. In an impressionistic assessment and explanation of the work he has written:

> I have always thought of the Rotary as being a turntable, a cartwheel, a bottleneck extension, a continuation of the New Jersey Turnpike, a highway roundabout at the exit of the Holland Tunnel and the entrance to Manhattan…a scene of incessant change, a hub, a place of rush hour glut, a place of disorientation….Both the pedestrian and the driver retain a multiplicity of successive views. For the driver the multiplicity of views is embedded in an inseparable temporal and spatial continuum, whereas the pedestrian can parcel out images….Given this essential distinction, the experiences of driver and pedestrian are identical in that neither can ascribe the multiplicity of views to a Gestalt reading of the *Arc*. Its form remains ambiguous, indeterminable, unknowable.[20]

In acquiring and exhibiting public art by some of our most adventurous creative personalities, the Port Authority has put its convictions on the firing line. It has judiciously sought a balance of works by established artists and the emerging avant-garde, and clearly some of the art of quality it espouses poses a challenge to popular

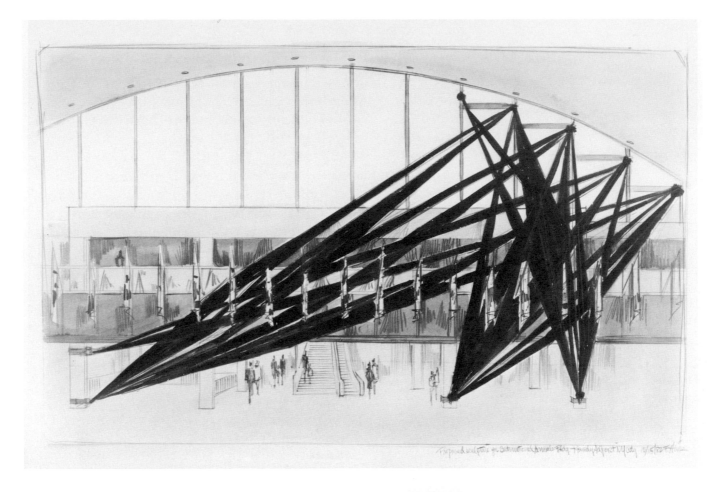

Francis Hines
Study for *Celebrating Flight* (Project for International Arrivals Building, Kennedy International Airport). 1982
Installation celebrating 25th anniversary of building

Robert Irwin
Line Rectangle (Project for the World Trade Center). 1977
On-site installation in conjunction with exhibition at Whitney Museum of American Art

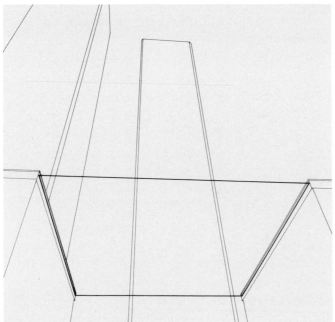

taste and even to public good will. Whatever its formal content or intellectual accessibility for the general populace, however, large-scale sculpture in public places has obvious charisma today. It touches an age-old need to rally the community around visible symbols of its shared purpose. Western society has progressively enfeebled and degraded the sense of community, and current assaults on the integrity of the environment further compound the problem, intensifying feelings of alienation. Thanks to the courage and scope of the activities of the Port Authority and similiar agencies, public art in all mediums has today succeeded in engaging artists and a mass audience in a fresh dialogue, raising critical issues of patronage and taste that have not been seriously broached since the heyday of the socially innovative WPA Federal Art Program.

NOTES

1/ Hailed by journalist Harrison Salisbury as "the world's most modern air terminal" when dedicated on Dec. 5, 1957 (*The New York Times*, Dec. 6, 1957, p. 1), the building designed by Gordon Bunshaft of Skidmore, Owings & Merrill was described by a travel writer for the *Times* (Dec. 8, 1957, Sec. 20, p. 3), as an "aesthetically satisfactory compromise." Although he did not take note of the Calder, it was reproduced with the caption: "Flight—Calder Mobile Sets the Airport Theme."

2/ This sculpture had been commissioned in 1965 by the architectural firm Skidmore, Owings & Merrill, responsible for the Civic Center's design.

3/ From Milton W. Brown et al, *American Art* (Englewood Cliffs, New Jersey: Prentice-Hall, 1978), p. 313.

4/ Saul Wenegrat in conversation with the author, June 1982.

5/ The current members are Dorothy C. Miller; Mrs. Charles W. Engelhard; Samuel C. Miller, Director of The Newark Museum; Thomas M. Messer, Director of The Solomon R. Guggenheim Museum, New York; Alan Sagner, Chairman of the Port Authority; Robert F. Wagner, Vice Chairman of the Port Authority and former Mayor of New York City; and Peter C. Goldmark, Jr., Executive Director of the Port Authority.

6/ The General Services Administration stipulates that one-half of one percent of the construction cost of a new Federal building may be expended for artwork. The State of New Jersey permits up to one and one-half percent of the construction cost of a new building with public access to be used for commissioning works of art. The State of New York has no percent-for-art enactment, but New York City in 1983 legislated that one percent of a new building's construction costs can be expended for art.

7/ The two panels were the focus of the exhibition "Murals without Walls: Arshile Gorky's Aviation Murals Rediscovered," at The Newark Museum, Newark, New Jersey, in 1978; Ruth Bowman was Guest Curator. Essays by Francis V. O'Connor, Ms. Bowman, and Jim M. Jordan discuss the murals and their recovery in detail. Samuel C. Miller, member of the Port Authority Committee on Art and Director of The Newark Museum, wrote the foreword to the catalog for this exhibition.

8/ In "My Murals for The Newark Airport: An Interpretation," written at the invitation of Emanuel Benson in 1936 for inclusion in what was to have been a national report on the WPA called *Art for the Millions*. Reprinted in Newark catalog, *ibid.*, pp. 13, 15–16.

9/ Alfred H. Barr, Jr., letter to Olive M. Lyford, WPA Federal Art Project, Oct. 14, 1936, quoted in Ethel K. Schwabacher, *Arshile Gorky* (New York: Macmillan, 1957), p. 76.

10/ In 1939, according to *Art News* (New York), vol. 39 (Nov. 11, 1939), when the Emergency Relief Appropriation Act was passed, New York City assumed jurisdiction for artist-relief projects within its borders.

11/ *Wall Street Journal* (New York), May 15, 1973.

12/ Edward Alden Jewell, "Flight Mural Installed at Airport," *The New York Times* (Sept. 20, 1942).

13/ Quoted in ibid.

14/ The sculpture was first placed on West Street, at the traffic entrance to the World Trade Center, in 1974. When the elevated West Side Highway was demolished, however, the site proved infelicitous and the work was moved in 1979 to its present location at the corner of Church and Vesey streets.

15/ The Port Authority News Release No. 233-78 (Dec. 12, 1978).

16/ Author's conversations with Mrs. Nevelson, 1982.

17/ Jan van der Marck, *George Segal* (New York: Abrams, 1975), p. 204.

18/ Sam Hunter, "Public Sculpture," *National Arts Guide*, May/June, 1980.

19/ Ibid.

20/ Richard Serra, "St. John's Rotary Arc," *Artforum* (New York), Sept. 1980, pp. 52–55.

Airports

The urge to fly has inspired three of the most monumental and most original works of art in the Port Authority collection. Two, vastly different in medium, are entitled *Flight:* Alexander Calder's airborne mobile, 1957 (frontispiece and back cover), suspended in the Main Hall of the International Arrivals Building at John F. Kennedy International Airport, and James Brooks's circular mural, 1940–42 (pages 60–61), installed at the Marine Air Terminal of LaGuardia Airport, where it provides a visual history of the vehicles of flight. The Calder was commissioned by the Port Authority for the opening of the Arrivals Building in 1957, and the Brooks mural was commissioned by the New York City Work Projects Administration (WPA) for LaGuardia Airport in 1940, a year after its opening. The third work was also commissioned by the WPA: Arshile Gorky's mural cycle for Newark Airport, *Aviation: Evolution of Forms under Aerodynamic Limitations,* 1936–37. Only two of ten panels survive: *Aerial Map* (page 58) and *Mechanics of Flying* (page 59), and they are on extended loan to The Newark Museum.

The two mural cycles were reclaimed from darkness through the intervention of the Port Authority art committee. Gorky's murals had been painted over by the Army Air Corps when it took command of the airport during World War II. Brooks's mural met a similar fate in the fifties, when WPA murals were at a low ebb in popularity. Recognized as two of the major undertakings of the WPA Mural Project, Gorky's and Brooks's paintings were restored in the seventies.

Another major program of the committee came about when Kennedy Airport's International Arrivals Building was enlarged in 1969. The art committee acquired a group of paintings, sculptures, tapestries, and prints to grace its long corridors (see map, pages 62–63; in captions for pages 64–85, numbers in parentheses refer to map locations).

Hans Hokanson
Helixikos, No. 18A. 1971
Carved wood,
39" x 24" x 24";
including base, 70" high
John F. Kennedy
International Airport
International Arrivals
Building (31)

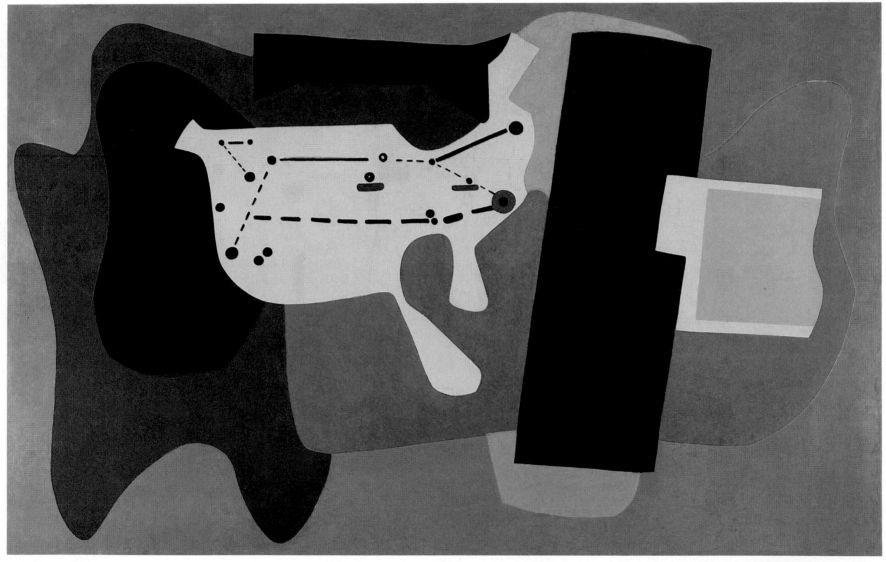

Arshile Gorky
*Aviation: Evolution of
Forms under Aerodynamic
Limitations: Aerial Map.*
1936–37
Oil on canvas, 77" x 10' 1"
On extended loan to The
Newark Museum,
Newark, New Jersey

Arshile Gorky
*Aviation: Evolution of
Forms under Aerodynamic
Limitations: Mechanics of
Flying.* 1936–37
Oil on canvas, 108″ x 11′1″
On extended loan to The
Newark Museum,
Newark, New Jersey

Marine Air Terminal, LaGuardia Airport

James Brooks
Flight. 1940–42
Casein-glyptol emulsion
on gessoed Belgian linen
mounted on wall,
12′ x 235′
Rotunda of Marine Air
Terminal, LaGuardia
Airport

Details, from left:
*Flight Accomplished:
Arrival of the Pam Am
Clipper*

Imagined Flight

Flight of Icarus

John F. Kennedy International Airport

International Arrivals Building, Second Floor

Index to Location of Art

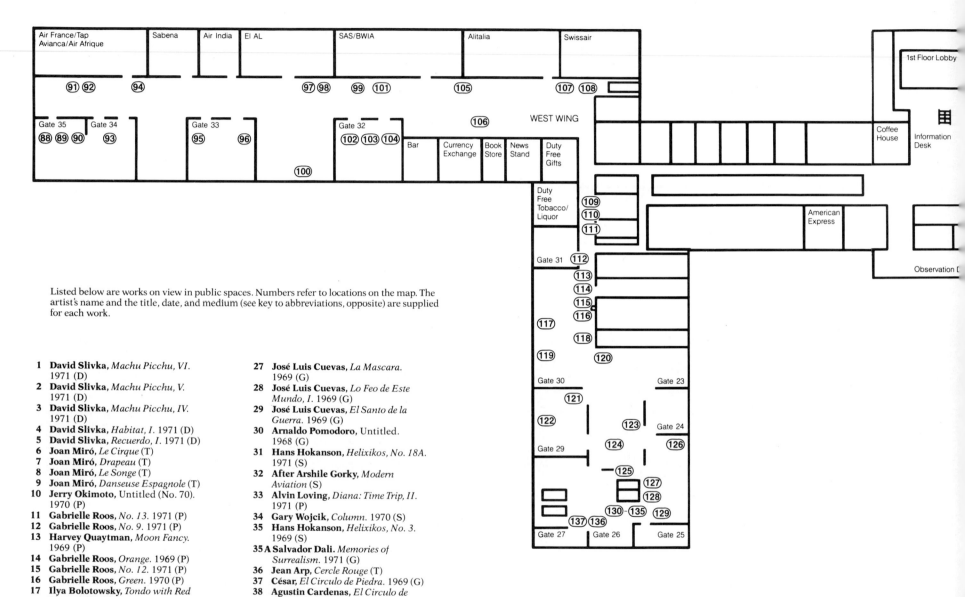

Listed below are works on view in public spaces. Numbers refer to locations on the map. The artist's name and the title, date, and medium (see key to abbreviations, opposite) are supplied for each work.

1 **David Slivka,** *Machu Picchu, VI.* 1971 (D)
2 **David Slivka,** *Machu Picchu, V.* 1971 (D)
3 **David Slivka,** *Machu Picchu, IV.* 1971 (D)
4 **David Slivka,** *Habitat, I.* 1971 (D)
5 **David Slivka,** *Recuerdo, I.* 1971 (D)
6 **Joan Miró,** *Le Cirque* (T)
7 **Joan Miró,** *Drapeau* (T)
8 **Joan Miró,** *Le Songe* (T)
9 **Joan Miró,** *Danseuse Espagnole* (T)
10 **Jerry Okimoto,** Untitled (No. 70). 1970 (P)
11 **Gabrielle Roos,** *No. 13.* 1971 (P)
12 **Gabrielle Roos,** *No. 9.* 1971 (P)
13 **Harvey Quaytman,** *Moon Fancy.* 1969 (P)
14 **Gabrielle Roos,** *Orange.* 1969 (P)
15 **Gabrielle Roos,** *No. 12.* 1971 (P)
16 **Gabrielle Roos,** *Green.* 1970 (P)
17 **Ilya Bolotowsky,** *Tondo with Red Plane.* 1970 (P)
18 **Ilya Bolotowsky,** *Pale Yellow and Blue Tondo.* 1970 (P)
19 **Ilya Bolotowsky,** *Dynamic Asymmetry.* 1970 (P)
20 **Luis Molinari-Flores,** *Construction, No. 28.* 1970 (P)
21 **Caroline Mackenzie,** *Green.* 1969 (P)
22 **Gloria Greenberg,** *Four Panels: No. 1.* 1971 (P)
23 **Gloria Greenberg,** *Four Panels: No. 2.* 1971 (P)
24 **Gloria Greenberg,** *Four Panels: No. 3.* 1971 (P)
25 **Gloria Greenberg,** *Four Panels: No. 4.* 1971 (P)
26 **Joseph Wilder,** *Graham Hill at Watkins Glen.* 1971. (P)

27 **José Luis Cuevas,** *La Mascara.* 1969 (G)
28 **José Luis Cuevas,** *Lo Feo de Este Mundo, I.* 1969 (G)
29 **José Luis Cuevas,** *El Santo de la Guerra.* 1969 (G)
30 **Arnaldo Pomodoro,** Untitled. 1968 (G)
31 **Hans Hokanson,** *Helixikos, No. 18A.* 1971 (S)
32 **After Arshile Gorky,** *Modern Aviation* (S)
33 **Alvin Loving,** *Diana: Time Trip, II.* 1971 (P)
34 **Gary Wojcik,** *Column.* 1970 (S)
35 **Hans Hokanson,** *Helixikos, No. 3.* 1969 (S)
35A **Salvador Dali.** *Memories of Surrealism.* 1971 (G)
36 **Jean Arp,** *Cercle Rouge* (T)
37 **César,** *El Circulo de Piedra.* 1969 (G)
38 **Agustin Cardenas,** *El Circulo de Piedra.* 1969 (G)
39 **Emilio Vedova,** *El Circulo de Piedra.* 1969 (G)
40 **Wifredo Lam,** *El Circulo de Piedra.* 1969 (G)
41 **Corneille,** *El Circulo de Piedra.* 1969 (G)
42 **Piotr Kowalski,** *El Circulo de Piedra.* 1969 (G)
43 **Edouard Pignon,** *El Circulo de Piedra.* 1969 (G)
44 **Valerio Adami,** *El Circulo de Piedra.* 1969 (G)
45 **Joan Miró,** *El Circulo de Piedra.* 1969 (G)
46 **Antoní Tapiès Puig,** *El Circulo de Piedra.* 1969 (G)
47 **Jorge Camacho,** *El Circulo de Piedra.* 1969 (G)

48 **Asger Jorn,** *El Circulo de Piedra.* 1969 (G)
49 **Alexander Calder,** *El Circulo de Piedra.* 1969 (G)
50 **Paul Rebeyrolle,** *El Circulo de Piedra.* 1969 (G)
51 **Erro,** *El Circulo de Piedra.* 1969 (G)
52 **Alexander Calder,** *Far West.* 1968 (G)
53 **Gerhardt Liebmann,** *Summer Rain at Sea.* 1971 (P)
54 **Alfons Schilling,** *Washington, II.* 1969–70 (P)
55 **David Slivka,** Untitled. 1964 (D)
56 **David Slivka,** *Brahmin.* 1971 (D)
57 **David Slivka,** *Juggernaut, I.* 1971 (D)
58 **David Slivka,** *Phoenix.* 1970 (D)

59 **Gerhardt Liebmann,** *Abyss.* 1971 (P)
60 **John Salt,** *Skylark.* 1969 (P)
61 **Clinton J. Hill,** *Uneven Sequence.* 1967 (P)
62 **Edward Corbett,** *Washington, D.C., October 1964, No. 8.* 1964 (P)
63 **Edward Corbett,** *Provincetown, 1968, No. 7.* 1968 (P)
64 **Terry Taggart,** *CN 1677.* 1970 (P)
65 **William M. Gilchrist,** *Birth of a New Style.* 1970 (P)
66 **Janet Fish,** *Vinegar Bottles.* 1972 (P)
67 **Janet Fish,** *Windex Bottles.* 1971–72 (P)
68 **Janet Fish,** *Two Boxes of Lemons.* 1970 (P)

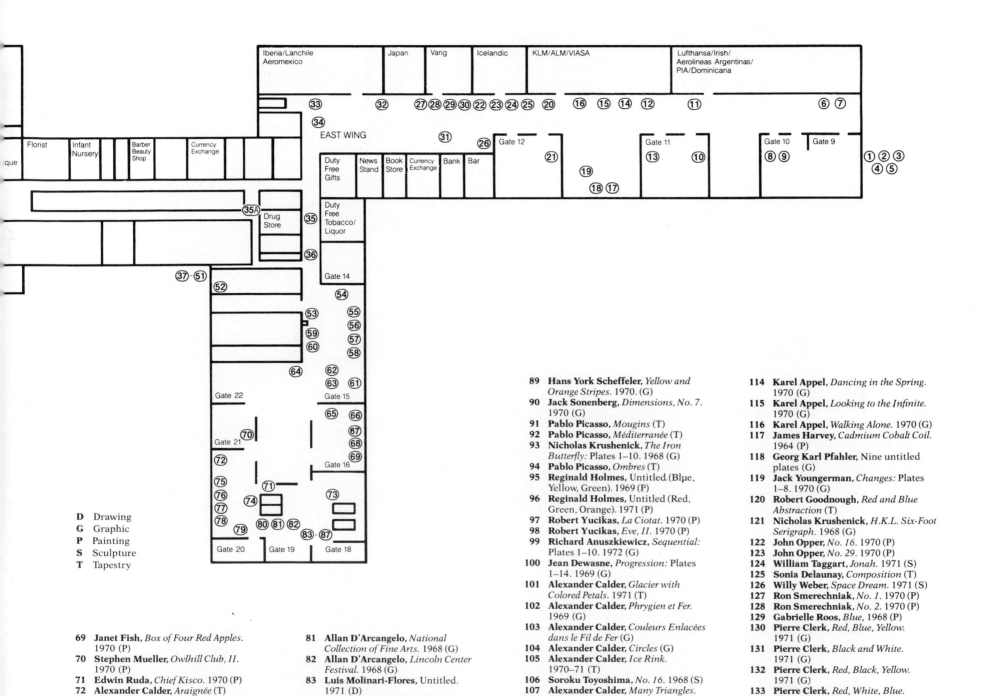

Iberia/Lanchile Aeromexico | Japan | Varig | Icelandic | KLM/ALM/VIASA | Lufthansa/Irish/ Aerolineas Argentinas/ PIA/Dominicana

EAST WING

Florist | Infant Nursery | Barber Beauty Shop | Currency Exchange

Duty Free Gifts | News Stand | Book Store | Currency Exchange | Bank | Bar

Gate 12 | Gate 11 | Gate 10 | Gate 9

Drug Store

Duty Free Tobacco/ Liquor

Gate 14

Gate 22 | Gate 21 | Gate 20 | Gate 19 | Gate 18 | Gate 16 | Gate 15

D Drawing
G Graphic
P Painting
S Sculpture
T Tapestry

69 **Janet Fish,** *Box of Four Red Apples.* 1970 (P)
70 **Stephen Mueller,** *Owlhill Club, II.* 1970 (P)
71 **Edwin Ruda,** *Chief Kisco.* 1970 (P)
72 **Alexander Calder,** *Araignée* (T)
73 **Alexander Calder,** *Femme Arabe.* 1970–71 (T)
74 **Courroy,** *Nervures* (T)
75 **Lothar Quinte,** *Luna Blue* (G)
76 **Lothar Quinte,** *Blue Luna* (G)
77 **Lothar Quinte,** *Silver Luna* (G)
78 **Lothar Quinte,** *Luna Silver* (G)
79 **Ilya Bolotowsky,** *Red and White.* 1964 (P)
80 **John Button,** *San Francisco Hill.* 1968 (P)
81 **Allan D'Arcangelo,** *National Collection of Fine Arts.* 1968 (G)
82 **Allan D'Arcangelo,** *Lincoln Center Festival.* 1968 (G)
83 **Luis Molinari-Flores,** *Untitled.* 1971 (D)
84 **Luis Molinari-Flores,** *New York Downtown.* 1971 (D)
85 **Luis Molinari-Flores,** *After Construction, No. 28.* 1970 (D)
86 **Luis Molinari-Flores,** *Gama Amarillo Azul.* 1970 (D)
87 **Luis Molinari-Flores,** *Salacas.* 1970 (D)
88 **Hans York Scheffeler,** *Blue, Purple, Green Stripes.* 1970 (G)

89 **Hans York Scheffeler,** *Yellow and Orange Stripes.* 1970. (G)
90 **Jack Sonenberg,** *Dimensions, No. 7.* 1970 (G)
91 **Pablo Picasso,** *Mougins* (T)
92 **Pablo Picasso,** *Méditerranée* (T)
93 **Nicholas Krushenick,** *The Iron Butterfly:* Plates 1–10. 1968 (G)
94 **Pablo Picasso,** *Ombres* (T)
95 **Reginald Holmes,** Untitled (Blue, Yellow, Green). 1969 (P)
96 **Reginald Holmes,** Untitled (Red, Green, Orange). 1971 (P)
97 **Robert Yucikas,** *La Ciotat.* 1970 (P)
98 **Robert Yucikas,** *Eve, II.* 1970 (P)
99 **Richard Anuszkiewicz,** *Sequential:* Plates 1–10. 1972 (G)
100 **Jean Dewasne,** *Progression:* Plates 1–14. 1969 (G)
101 **Alexander Calder,** *Glacier with Colored Petals.* 1971 (T)
102 **Alexander Calder,** *Phrygien et Fer.* 1969 (G)
103 **Alexander Calder,** *Couleurs Enlacées dans le Fil de Fer* (G)
104 **Alexander Calder,** *Circles* (G)
105 **Alexander Calder,** *Ice Rink.* 1970–71 (T)
106 **Soroku Toyoshima,** *No. 16.* 1968 (S)
107 **Alexander Calder,** *Many Triangles.* 1970–71 (T)
108 **Alexander Calder,** *Spirales.* 1970–71 (T)
109 **Kyohei Inukai,** *Triangloform, XI.* c. 1970 (P)
110 **Kyohei Inukai,** *Triangloform, IX.* c. 1970 (P)
111 **Pierre Clerk,** *Delancey Street.* 1970 (P)
112 **Pierre Clerk,** *Houston Street.* 1970 (P)
113 **Karel Appel,** *Dream-Colored Head.* 1970 (G)

114 **Karel Appel,** *Dancing in the Spring.* 1970 (G)
115 **Karel Appel,** *Looking to the Infinite.* 1970 (G)
116 **Karel Appel,** *Walking Alone.* 1970 (G)
117 **James Harvey,** *Cadmium Cobalt Coil.* 1964 (P)
118 **Georg Karl Pfahler,** Nine untitled plates (G)
119 **Jack Youngerman,** *Changes:* Plates 1–8. 1970 (G)
120 **Robert Goodnough,** *Red and Blue Abstraction* (T)
121 **Nicholas Krushenick,** *H.K.L. Six-Foot Serigraph.* 1968 (G)
122 **John Opper,** *No. 16.* 1970 (P)
123 **John Opper,** *No. 29.* 1970 (P)
124 **William Taggart,** *Jonah.* 1971 (S)
125 **Sonia Delaunay,** *Composition* (T)
126 **Willy Weber,** *Space Dream.* 1971 (S)
127 **Ron Smerechniak,** *No. 1.* 1970 (P)
128 **Ron Smerechniak,** *No. 2.* 1970 (P)
129 **Gabrielle Roos,** *Blue,* 1968 (P)
130 **Pierre Clerk,** *Red, Blue, Yellow.* 1971 (G)
131 **Pierre Clerk,** *Black and White.* 1971 (G)
132 **Pierre Clerk,** *Red, Black, Yellow.* 1971 (G)
133 **Pierre Clerk,** *Red, White, Blue.* 1971 (G)
134 **Pierre Clerk,** *Black and White.* 1970 (G)
135 **Pierre Clerk,** *Black and White.* 1970 (G)
136 **Doug Ohlson,** *Champ, No. 54.* 1971 (P)
137 **J. C. Pass Fearrington,** Untitled. 1970 (P)

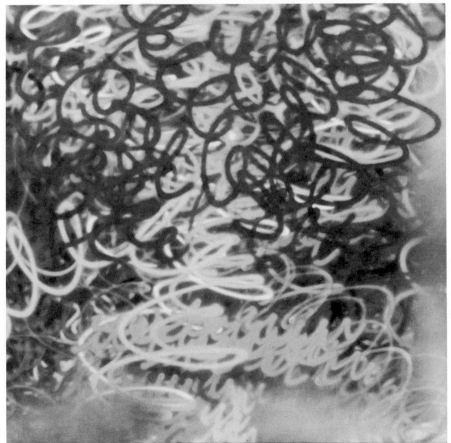

Above left:
Joseph Wilder
Graham Hill at Watkins Glen. 1971
Oil on canvas, 72" x 48"
IAB (26)

Above right:
Alan Samalin
Picturing Flight (detail).
1982
Acrylic on canvas,
IAB (Control Tower)

Right:
David Cummings
Holmul. 1970
Acrylic on canvas,
60" x 60"
IAB (VIP Lounge)

Opposite, left:
Edward Corbett
Washington, D.C., October 1964, No. 8. 1964
Oil on canvas, 60" x 50"
IAB (62)

Opposite, right:
David Slivka
Untitled. August 11, 1964
Brush and ink on paper,
40" x 26"
IAB (55)

Above left:
John Button
San Francisco Hill. 1968
Oil on canvas, 60″ x 48″
IAB (80)

Below left:
Alvin Loving
Diana: Time Trip, II. 1971
Acrylic on canvas,
89″ x 20′8″
IAB (33)

Left:
Hans Hokanson
Serpent. 1976
Elm wood, 71″ x 24″ x 22″

Bob Duran
Untitled. c. 1971
Acrylic on canvas,
68" x 100"
IAB (In Transit Lounge)

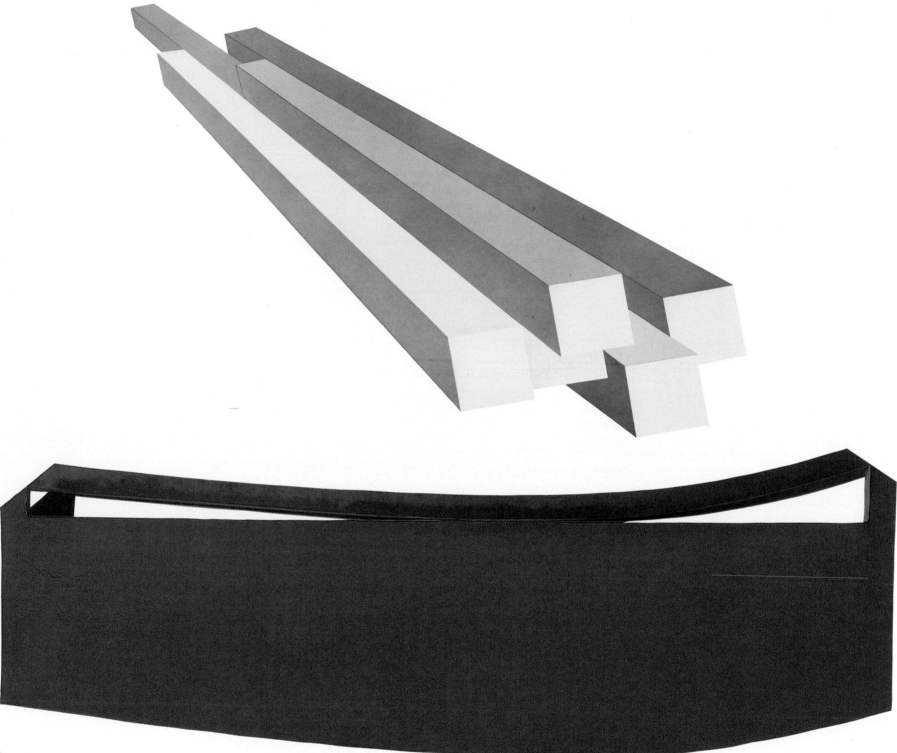

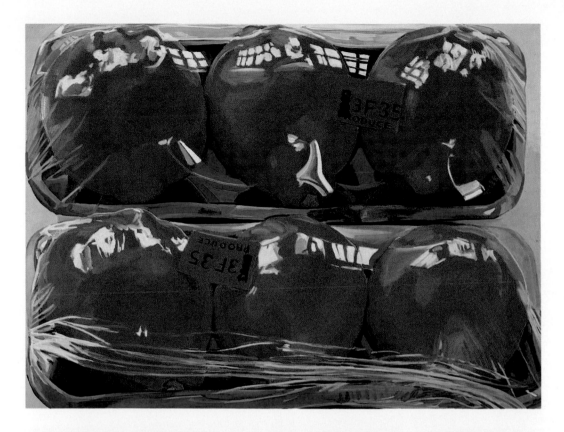

Opposite, top:
Jerry Okimoto
Untitled (No. 70). 1970
Acrylic on canvas,
36″ x 108″
IAB (10)

Opposite, bottom:
Harvey Quaytman
Moon Fancy. 1969
Acrylic and dry pigment
on canvas, 38″ x 109″
IAB (13)

Top left:
Janet Fish
Two Boxes of Lemons.
1970
Oil on linen, 36″ x 48″
IAB (68)

Bottom left:
Janet Fish
Vinegar Bottles. 1972
Oil on linen, 50″ x 60″
IAB (66)

Above:
Pablo Picasso
Jacqueline
Cut-pile wool tapestry,
70¾" x 90½"

Below:
John Opper
No. 16. 1970
Acrylic on canvas,
54" x 66"
IAB (122)

Opposite, above left:
Valerio Adami
Untitled plate from
*El Circulo de Piedra
(Circle of Stone).* 1969
Lithograph,
17¾" x 22¼"
IAB (44)

Opposite, above right:
Nicholas Krushenick
Plate from
The Iron Butterfly. 1968
Serigraph on rag board
(46/125), 35½" x 27½"
IAB (93)

Opposite, below left:
Marja Vallila
Elevated Plaza. 1980
Steel and copper,
54" x 38" x 20"

Opposite, below right:
Alfons Schilling
Washington, II. 1969–70
Photoemulsion on lenticular, transparent plastic
screen, 67¾" x 59¼"
IAB (54)

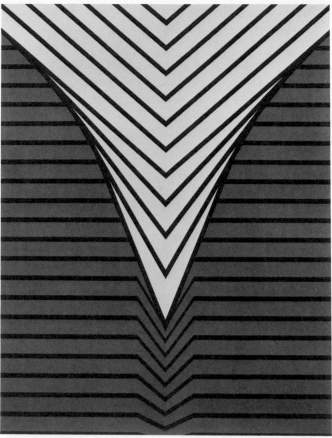

Ilya Bolotowsky
*Pale Yellow and Blue
Tondo.* 1970
Acrylic on canvas,
46″ diameter
IAB (18)

Opposite:
Robert Goodnough
Red and Blue Abstraction
1970
Flatweave wool tapestry
(1/5), 77″ x 103″
IAB (120)

Sonia Delaunay
Composition
Aubusson tapestry
(unique),
70″ x 112″
IAB (125)

Opposite, top:
John Salt
Skylark. 1969
Oil on canvas, 53″ x 69″
IAB (60)

Opposite, bottom:
José Guerrero
Zoco. 1969
Oil on canvas, 54″ x 61″

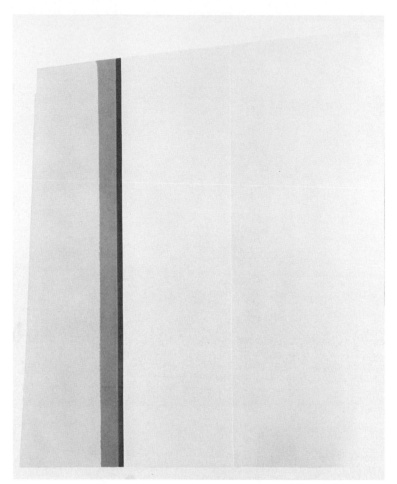

Above:
Clinton J. Hill
Uneven Sequence. 1967
Oil on canvas, 68″ x 55″
IAB (61)

Below left:
Robert Johannes Sindorf
Times Past. 1981
Italian white marble,
36″ x 18″ x 4″; including
base, 74″ high

Below right:
Alexander Calder
Many Triangles. 1970–71
Aubusson tapestry,
52″ x 80″
IAB (107)

Opposite:
Gabrielle Roos
No. 13. 1971
Acrylic on canvas,
48″ x 90″
IAB (11)

Opposite:
Alexander Calder
Femme Arabe (Arab Woman), 1970–71
Aubusson tapestry,
78″ x 54″
IAB (73)

Left:
Edward Corbett
Provincetown, 1968, No. 7
1968
Oil on canvas, 60″ x 50″
IAB (63)

Right:
Jack Youngerman
Plate 2 from *Changes*
1970
Serigraph (163/175),
43″ x 33″
IAB (119)

Below:
Del Geist
Cudjoe, II. 1977
Cor-Ten steel,
44″ x 56″ x 92″

Opposite, top left:
Kyohei Inukai
Triangloform, IX. c. 1970
Acrylic on canvas,
50″ x 60″
IAB (110)

Opposite, top right:
José Luis Cuevas
La Mascara (The Mask)
1969
Embossed lithograph
with gold acetate
(24/100), 30″ x 22″
IAB (27)

Opposite, bottom:
Victoria Barr
Vent. 1971
Acrylic on canvas,
62″ x 69″

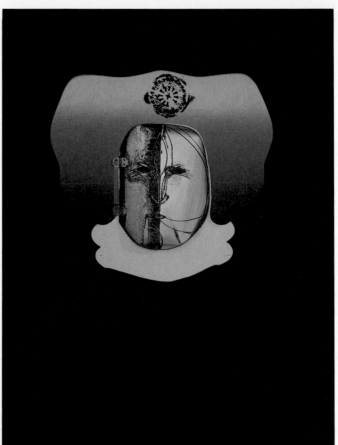
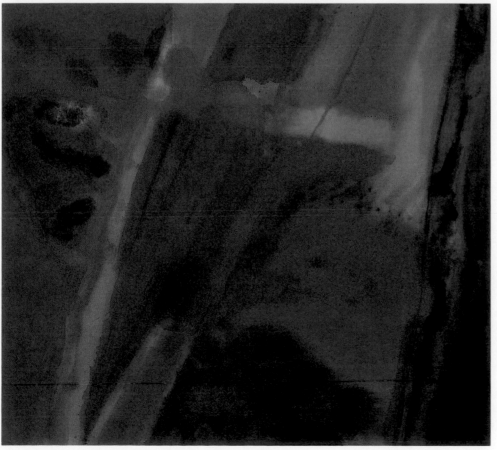

Opposite:
Edwin Ruda
Chief Kisco. 1970
Acrylic on canvas,
70″ x 90″
IAB (71)

Left:
Gerhardt Liebmann
Summer Rain at Sea. 1971
Acrylic on canvas,
86″ x 84″
IAB (53)

Port Authority Bus Terminal

J. Esteban Perez
*Constructivist Space
Drawing.* 1981
Fifteen fired-porcelain
enamel panels on 40-
gauge steel; 13 panels,
each 34″ x 34″ x 3″; end
panels, each 34″ x 48″ x 3″
Port Authority Bus
Terminal (B Level)

Right:
George Rhoads
42nd Street Ballroom.
1983
Kinetic sculpture,
96″ x 96″ x 96″
Port Authority Bus
Terminal (South Wing)

Opposite:
Richard Anuszkiewicz
Complimentary Gothic, I.
1984
Series of 12 silkscreen
double-faced banners,
12′ x 48″
Port Authority Bus Ter-
minal (South Wing)

World Trade Center

The Port Authority of New York and New Jersey commissioned the architect Minoru Yamasaki to create a building complex in lower Manhattan to bring together businesses and organizations involved in international trade, thereby expanding the bistate port's activity in that area. The twin 110-story buildings command a view of New York Harbor and the Statue of Liberty. Connecting the two buildings is a five-acre plaza sloping down in the center to a fountain surmounted by a bronze spherical sculpture, 1969 (opposite), designed by German sculptor Fritz Koenig. Also located in the plaza are Japanese sculptor Masayuki Nagare's granite work, 1972 (page 99), and James Rosati's Constructivist *Ideogram*, 1974 (page 21). As monumental in scale are two works hanging on the walls of the mezzanine lobbies of towers one and two: Louise Nevelson's *Sky Gate, New York*, 1977–78 (page 95), and Joan Miró's *World Trade Center Tapestry*, 1974 (page 7). Outside the plaza proper but tucked under the corner of a building in the Trade Center complex is Alexander Calder's red *World Trade Center Stabile*, 1971 (page 32).

The World Trade Center houses the executive offices of the Port Authority, as well as restaurants such as Windows on the World. Placed throughout the spaces are paintings, sculptures, prints, posters, tapestries, and textiles, many of which appear on the pages that follow.

Fritz Koenig
Sphere for Plaza Fountain
1969
Bronze (unique cast, 1970–71) on black-granite base, 25' high
Austin J. Tobin Plaza

Opposite:
Kenneth Snelson
Needle Tower. 1968
Aluminum and stainless
steel wire, 96″ high
Windows on the World

Le Corbusier
Nature Morte
Aubusson tapestry,
88″ x 11′7½″

Kenneth Noland
Nizhoni Peak
Navajo flatweave wool
tapestry, 70″ x 70″
Windows on the World

Opposite:
Masayuki Nagare
*World Trade Center Plaza
Sculpture.* 1972
Black Swedish granite
over steel armature,
14′ x 34′ x 17′; base,
33′6″ long x 15′9⅞″ wide
Austin J. Tobin Plaza

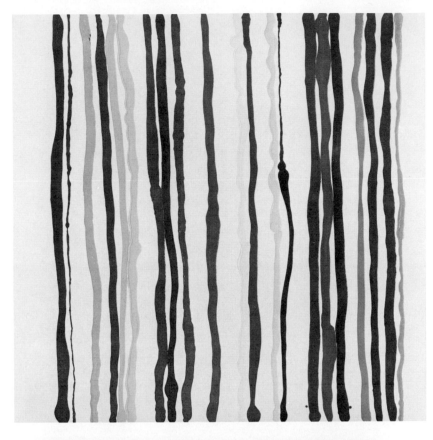

Opposite, above:
Wendy Jeffers
No. 30. 1975
Acrylic and Rhoplex on canvas, 72″ x 72″

Opposite, below left:
D. Harrison Burns
Hunterdon County. c. 1975
Acrylic on canvas,
60″ x 72″

Opposite, below right:
Ulaaq Ahvakana
Have You Ever Danced for What You Eat?
Vermont marble
with ivory,
28½″ x 22″ x 3¼″

Above:
Marina Stern
George Washington Bridge, Nos. 1 and 2
1971
Oil on two canvas panels,
each 58″ x 36″

Below:
Paul Klee
Bleu-Rouge (Blue-Red)
Cut-pile wool tapestry,
59″ x 76¾″
World Trade Institute

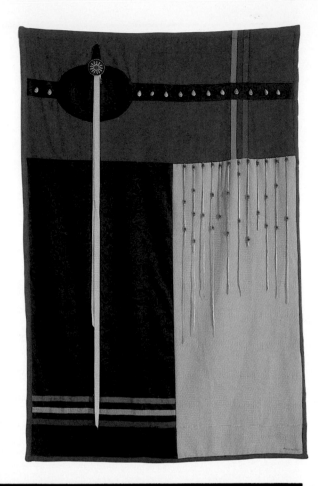

Above:
Arthur Amiotte
Woman's Dress
Wall hanging of leather,
beads, and fabric,
75″ x 50½″

Right:
Le Corbusier
*Les Dés Sont Jetés (The
Throw of the Dice)*
Aubusson tapestry,
87½″ x 11′8″

Opposite:
Romare Bearden
Recollection Pond
Wool and cotton flat-
weave tapestry, 61″ x 75″
Windows on the World

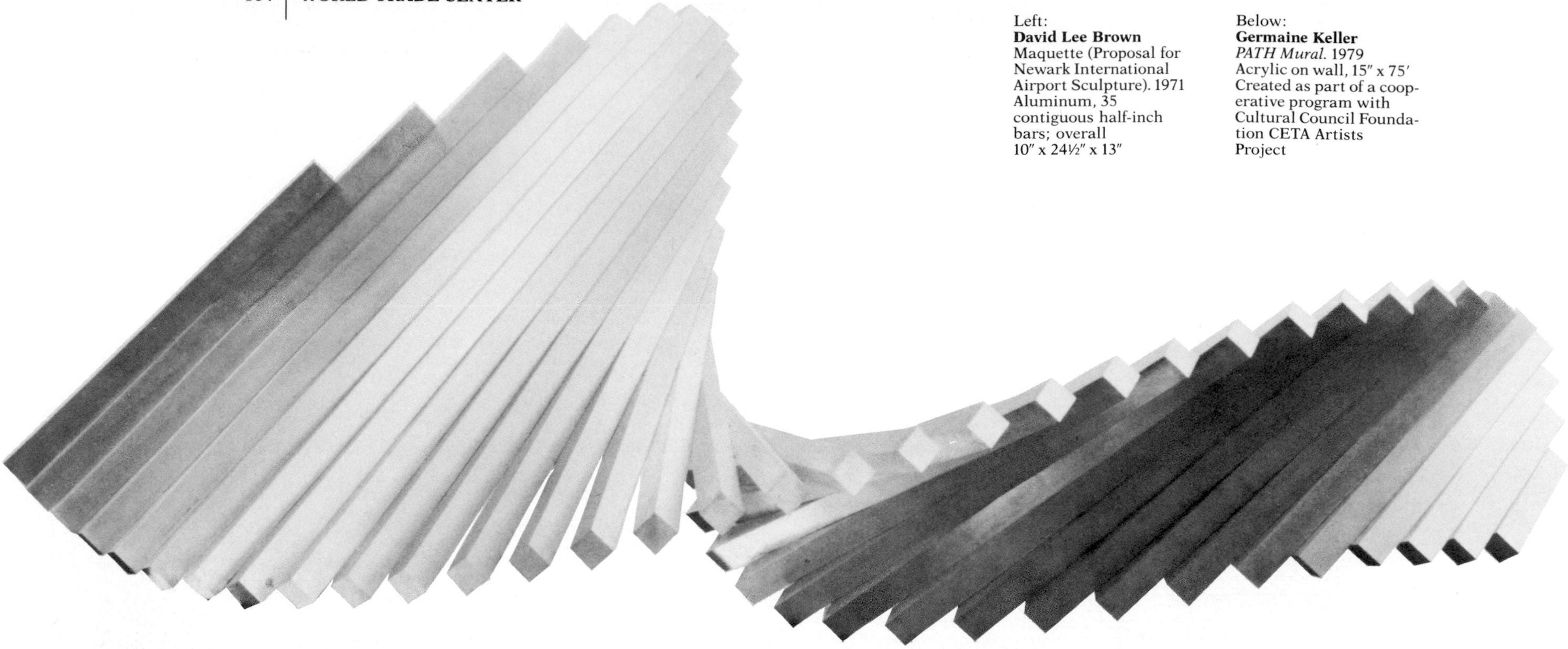

Left:
David Lee Brown
Maquette (Proposal for
Newark International
Airport Sculpture). 1971
Aluminum, 35
contiguous half-inch
bars; overall
10″ x 24½″ x 13″

Below:
Germaine Keller
PATH Mural. 1979
Acrylic on wall, 15″ x 75′
Created as part of a coop-
erative program with
Cultural Council Founda-
tion CETA Artists
Project

Above:
Robert Birmelin
*A Rocky Beach with a
Man Looking through
Binoculars.* 1972
Acrylic on canvas,
48″ x 48″

Bottom left:
Gerald Monroe
Grace Mary. 1973
Oil on canvas, 66″ x 60″

Bottom right:
Senufo Tribe (Dahomey)
Masked Figure
Wood, 36″ high

Above left:
Corneille
Untitled
Aubusson tapestry,
78″ x 50″

Above right:
George Constant
Love
Watercolor, 14½″ x 11″

Below left:
Masuo Ikeda
Landscape in the Day
Lithograph (23/55),
26½″ x 21½″

Below right:
Vittorio Ottanelli
*Spotlight Brown on Blue
Field.* 1974
Tapestry (6/73), 71″ x 51″

Above:
Frank Bowling
Untitled
Acrylic on canvas,
74" x 66"

Right:
Ronald Mallory
Cruise Ship Entering New York. 1982
Oil on canvas, 48" x 84"
Windows on the World

Below:
Tony King
Triangle. c. 1971
Oil on shaped canvas,
each side 60″

Right:
John Grillo
Bright Farm. 1973
Gouache, 22″ x 30″

Below right:
Susan Leites
Tulips. 1976
Oil on shaped canvas,
60″ x 36″
Windows on the World

Opposite, top left:
René Fumeron
Air Bleu
Aubusson tapestry,
77½″ x 48″

Opposite, top right:
Richard Haas
The Dakota. 1971
Drypoint (13/40),
19⅞″ x 24⅛″

Opposite, bottom:
Thelma Appel
Snow. 1972
Acrylic and oil on canvas,
36¾″ x 86″

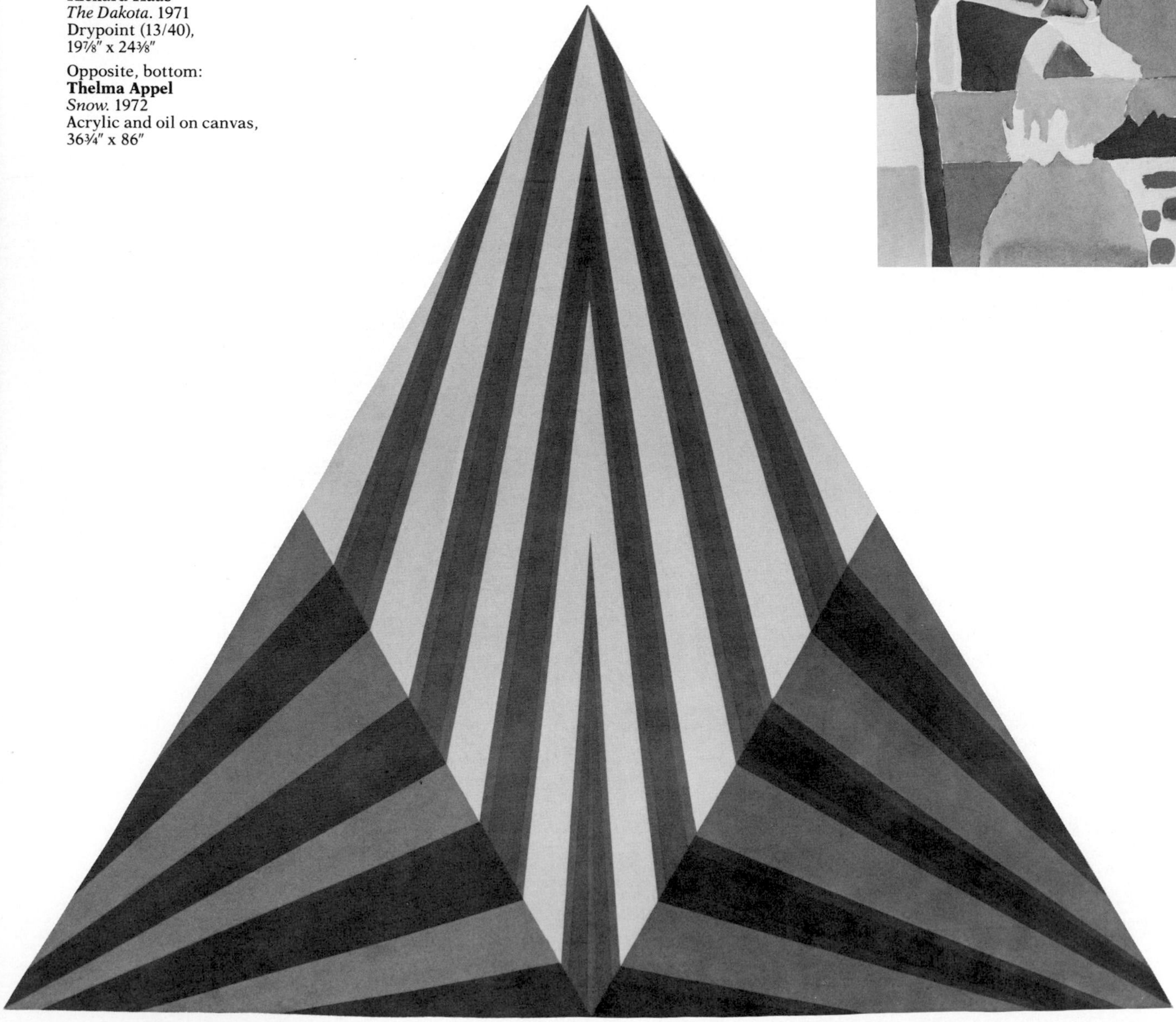

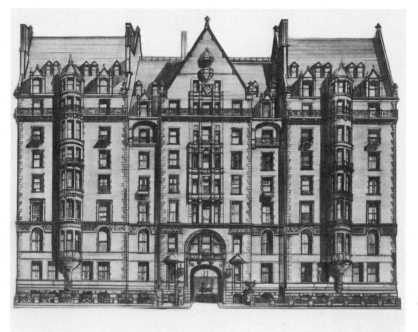

Above left:
Pierre Clerk
Orange, Brown, Blue. 1975
Mexican flatweave tapestry, 72″ diameter

Above right:
Kenneth Noland
Twilight
Navajo flatweave tapestry, 71″ x 71″
Windows on the World

Right:
Stan Brodsky
Seascape. 1974
Oil on canvas, 34″ x 44″

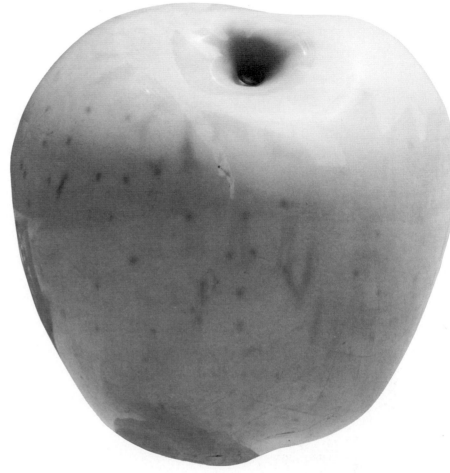

Above left:
Nancy Wissemann-Widrig
Director's Chair.
1971
Acrylic on canvas,
42″ x 50″

Above right:
Donn Moulton
Apple. 1973
Enamel on
molded fiberglass,
31″ x 30″ x 12″

Bottom:
Cynthia Mailman
Commuter Land-scape. 1979
Acrylic on canvas,
96″ x 53′
Created in cooper-
ation with the
Cultural Council
Foundation CETA
Artists Project
PATH (World
Trade Center Ter-
minal)

Checklist of the Collection

Editor's Note
Listed on the following pages are more than five hundred works of art from the Port Authority of New York and New Jersey collection. They are grouped in three sections: (1) Paintings, Sculptures, and Drawings; (2) Prints and Posters; and (3) Tapestries and Other Wall Hangings. Although the illustrations have been arranged according to location or facility, this list attempts to provide a coherent view of the entire collection by medium. The three sections are each arranged alphabetically by artist, chronologically for the works of a single artist.

Although most works acquired by the Committee on Art since its formation in 1969 have been signed and dated, some have not and no precise date can be assigned; the date of acquisition is given for all but a few works, however. The date for a sculpture in bronze refers to the original version in plaster or clay; wherever possible, the date of casting is also supplied. Certain works replicated after earlier maquettes are listed according to the date of replication. The few African works in the collection are undated; all were collected— and therefore probably made—in this century. The artists' titles are retained throughout, even those in a foreign language. The parenthetic translations are the editor's.

Dimensions are listed in feet and inches and in centimeters, height preceding width, followed by depth in the case of sculptures and constructions. Measurements are also given for bases made or specified by the sculptor. Sheet sizes are given for works on paper, unless otherwise noted.

The collection contains a substantial number of prints and posters, most dating from 1969 to the present. The printmaking medium, which has flourished since the fifteenth century, saw an explosion of techniques and styles in the post-World War II era, when the fine-art print enjoyed a level of popularity heretofore reserved to painting or sculpture. The serigraph (silkscreen) and lithography processes were used to produce hard-edge, geometric color prints, of which the Port Authority collection contains major examples. Because print publishers have played an innovative role in the production of the modern print, they are cited, if known, after the title and date of each print or poster. Limited editions are noted by the information given in parentheses (e.g., 2/100 refers to the second print pulled in an edition of 100).

The modern tapestry or wall hanging is particularly well represented in the collection, the outstanding example being the giant, unique work by Miró hanging in the lobby of Two World Trade Center. The ancient weaver's art took on modern overtones in the thirties, when the Frenchwoman, Marie Cuttoli, approached important artists of the School of Paris for original designs to be woven by the artisans of Aubusson, France, and elsewhere. They produced handmade work of the highest technical achievement. Since then the art has flourished not just in France but in other countries as well. It is not uncommon for a single design to be repeated a number of times, each piece made to order by meticulous craftsmen. Dates of the original designs are difficult to determine, so in most cases only the date of acquisition appears. Each tapestry was made at a date close to the time of acquisition, however.

The collection is located throughout the New York–New Jersey Metropolitan Region in the Port Authority's various facilities. These are identified in each listing in an abbreviated form, and the key to these abbreviations follows:

GWB	George Washington Bridge Bus Station Concourse	**LAG**	LaGuardia Airport Sites: Central Terminal Building Hangar 7, Conference Room Marine Air Terminal
HT	Holland Tunnel		
JFKIA	Kennedy International Airport, International Arrivals Building. Numbers in parentheses refer to map, pp. 62–63. The following sites do not appear on the map: Control Tower Main Hall, 1st Floor Security Office VIP Lounge West Wing, In Transit Lounge, 3rd Floor	**NIA**	Newark International Airport
		NYCPST	New York City Passenger Ship Terminal
		PABT	Port Authority Bus Terminal
		PATH	Port Authority Trans-Hudson Corp.
		WTC	World Trade Center General offices of The Port Authority of New York and New Jersey, One World Trade Center. Specific Locations: Austin J. Tobin Plaza Windows on the World World Trade Institute
JSTC	Journal Square Transportation Center, Jersey City, New Jersey		

Paintings/Sculptures/Drawings

AGAM, Yaacov
Israeli, born 1928. Works in Paris and Israel
Reflection and Depth. 1984
Acrylic on mirrored stainless steel, 20'7" x 19'6" (629.6 x 609 cm)
Commissioned 1981; installed 1984
PABT (North Wing)

AHVAKANA, Ulaaq (Lawrence Reynold)
American, born 1946
Have You Ever Danced for What You Eat? 1972
Vermont marble with ivory, 28½" x 22" x 3¼" (72.4 x 55.9 x 8.3 cm)
Acquired 1972
WTC

APPEL, Thelma
American, born Israel 1940
Snow. 1972
Acrylic and oil on canvas, 36¾" x 86" (93.3 x 218.4 cm)
Acquired 1973
WTC

ARP, Jean (Hans)
French, born Alsace. 1887–1966. In Switzerland 1959–66
Lettre Terrestre (Earthly Letter). 1970. Published by Librairie-Galerie La Hune, Paris
Gold-plated brass on lucite base (150/300), 5" x 5½" (12.7 x 14 cm)
Acquired 1970
WTC

BARNES, Alice
American
Orion
Wood relief with gold leaf, 48" x 30" (121.9 x 76.2 cm), two panels, each 102" x 72" (259.1 x 182.9 cm)
Acquired 1976
WTC (Windows)

Genesis. 1975
Oil on canvas, 40" x 50" (101.6 x 127 cm)
Acquired 1976
WTC

BARR, Victoria
American, born 1937
Vent. 1971
Acrylic on canvas, 62" x 69" (157.5 x 175.3 cm)
Acquired 1972
JFKIA

BASTIAN, Linda
American, born 1940
Night Orchids. 1981
Watercolor, 22½" x 30" (57.2 x 76.2 cm)
Acquired 1982
WTC

Tree Peony. 1981
Watercolor, 22½" x 30" (57.2 x 76.2 cm)
Acquired 1982
WTC

BATTERMAN, Lee
American
Boats. c. 1960
Oil on canvas, 40½" x 49" (102.9 x 124.5 cm)
Acquired 1975
WTC

BAULE TRIBE (Ivory Coast)
Wedding Masks
Carved polished wood; two, each 19" x 11" x 7" (48.2 x 27.9 x 17.8 cm)
Acquired 1983
GWB
Note: Representations of bride and groom

BEADLE, Peter
New Zealander
Landscape. (N.d.)
Oil on canvas, 24" x 36" (61 x 91.4 cm)
Acquired 1974, gift of the Government of New Zealand
JSTC

BECK, T. A. and I. W.
American
Eagle. c. 1939
Cast aluminum, 48" x 84" (121.9 x 213.4 cm)
WPA Federal Art Project
LAG (Hangar 7C Roof)
Note: Originally installed above entrance to Administration Building, LaGuardia Field, New York, 1939

BERGER, Robert
American
Late Summer. 1974
Acrylic on canvas, 52" x 65" (132.1 x 165.1 cm)
Acquired 1974
WTC

BIEDERMAN, James
American, born 1947
Vertumnus and Pomona (Study for *World Trade Center Mural*). 1979
Pencil on paper, 48½" x 98" (123.2 x 248.9 cm)
Acquired 1979
WTC

World Trade Center Mural. 1979
Oil and charcoal pencil on plasterboard wall, 93" x 16' 6" (236.2 x 503 cm)
Acquired 1979
WTC
Note: Created as part of a cooperative program with Cultural Council Foundation CETA Artists Project, with funds provided by the New York City Department of Employment

BIRMELIN, Robert
American, born 1933
A Rocky Beach with a Man Looking through Binoculars. 1972
Acrylic on canvas, 48" x 48" (121.9 x 121.9 cm)
Acquired 1974
WTC

BOLOTOWSKY, Ilya
American, born Russia. 1907–1981. To U.S. 1923
Red and White. 1964
Oil on canvas, 60" x 76" (152.4 x 195 cm)
Acquired 1971
JFKIA (79)

Dynamic Asymmetry. 1970
Acrylic on canvas, 44" x 44" (111.8 x 111.8 cm)
Acquired 1971
JFKIA (19)

Pale Yellow and Blue Tondo. 1970
Acrylic on canvas, 46" (116.8 cm) diameter
Acquired 1971
JFKIA (18)

Tondo with Red Plane. 1970
Acrylic on canvas, 38" (91.4 cm) diameter
Acquired 1971
JFKIA (17)

Maquette for *Marine Abstraction: Passenger Ship Terminal Mural*. 1978
Acrylic on wooden board, 5½" x 41" (14 x 104.1 cm)
Acquired 1979
WTC

*Marine Abstraction: Passenger Ship
Terminal Mural.* 1979
Ceramic tile, 48" x 40' (121.9 x 1,220 cm)
Acquired 1979 with funds provided in part
by the National Endowment for the Arts,
Washington D.C.
NYCPST (Term C)

BOSSON, Jack
American, born 1937
Zo May. 1970
Acrylic on canvas, 84" x 84"
(213.4 x 213.4 cm)
Acquired 1972
JFKIA

BOWLING, Frank
Guyanese, born 1936. To England 1959.
In U.S. 1967–76. Lives in England
Untitled. (N.d.)
Acrylic on canvas, 74" x 66"
(188 x 167.6 cm)
Acquired 1976
WTC

BRODSKY, Stan
American, born 1925
Seascape. 1974
Oil on canvas, 34" x 44" (86.4 x 111.8 cm)
Acquired 1976
WTC

Untitled. 1974
Oil on canvas, 40" x 50" (101.6 x 127 cm)
Acquired 1976
WTC

Ochre Shore. 1975
Oil on canvas, 42" x 52" (106.7 x 132.1 cm)
Acquired 1976
WTC

Slow Tide. 1975
Oil on canvas, 40" x 50" (101.6 x 127 cm)
Acquired 1976
WTC

BROOKS, James
American, born 1906
Flight. 1940–42
Mural for rotunda of Marine Air Terminal,
LaGuardia Airport
Casein-glyptol emulsion on gessoed
Belgian linen mounted on wall, 12' x 235'
(366 x 7,160 cm)
Commissioned by the New York City
Work Projects Administration (WPA) Art
Project, c. 1939; completed September 1942;
painted over c. 1952; restored 1979–80
with funds provided in part by
Laurance S. Rockefeller and DeWitt
Wallace
LAG (MAT)

BROWN, David Lee
American, born 1939
Maquette (Proposal for Newark
International Airport Sculpture). 1971
Aluminum form composed of 35
contiguous half-inch bars; overall
10" x 24½" x 13" (25.4 x 62.2 x 33 cm)
Acquired 1973
WTC

BURNS, D. Harrison
American, born 1946
Hunterdon County, c. 1975
Acrylic on canvas, 60" x 72"
(152.4 x 182.9 cm)
Acquired 1976
WTC

BUTCHKES, Sydney
American, born 1922
Untitled, No. 340. 1971
Acrylic on shaped canvas, 87" x 73" x 6"
(221 x 185.4 x 15.2 cm)
Acquired 1972
WTC

Untitled, No. 343. 1971
Acrylic on shaped canvas, 71" x 89" x 6"
(180.3 x 226.1 x 15.2 cm)
Acquired 1972
WTC

BUTTON, John
American, 1929–1982
San Francisco Hill. 1968
Oil on canvas, 60" x 48" (152.4 x 121.9 cm)
Acquired 1971
JFKIA (80)

CALDER, Alexander
American, 1898–1976
Lived in France and U.S.
Flight (.125). 1957
Painted-steel mobile, 45' (1,372 cm) wide
x 17' (518 cm) diameter
Acquired 1957
JFKIA (Main Hall)

The World Trade Center Stabile. 1971
Red painted steel, 25' (762 cm) high
Acquired 1971
Commissioned 1969; completed 1971;
installed West Street 1974; reinstalled
Church and Vesey Streets
WTC
Note: Executed after a 14'-high model,
black painted steel, called *Trois Ailes
(Three Wings)*

CHALIF, Ronnie
American
Untitled. (N.d.)
Stone, 14" (35.6 cm) high
Acquired 1973
WTC

CHINESE SCHOOL
Four Scenes of Birds and Flowers
19th Century
Brush and colored inks on silk mounted
on screen, each panel 44½" x 10¾"
(113 x 27.3 cm), image
Acquired 1977
WTC

CLERK, Pierre
American, born 1928. In Canada 1932–52.
In France 1952–54. In Italy 1954–59.
To U.S. 1959
Delancey Street. 1970
Acrylic on canvas, 49" x 47"
(124.5 x 119.4 cm)
Acquired 1971
JFKIA (111)

Houston Street. 1970
Acrylic on canvas, 72" (182.9 cm) diameter
Acquired 1971
JFKIA (112)

COIT, Madelin
American
Green Sea. 1981
Pastel on paper in nine parts, each
26" x 40" (66 x 101.6 cm); overall, 72" x 10'
(182.4 x 304 cm)
Acquired 1982
WTC

CONSTANT, George
American, born Greece. 1892–1978
Love. (N.d.)
Watercolor, 14½" x 11" (36.8 x 27.9 cm)
Acquired 1973
WTC

CORBETT, Edward
American, 1919–1971
Washington, D.C., October 1964, No. 8.
1964
Oil on canvas, 60" x 50" (152.4 x 127 cm)
Acquired 1972
JFKIA (62)

Provincetown, 1968, No. 7. 1968
Oil on canvas, 60" x 50" (152.4 x 127 cm)
Acquired 1972
JFKIA (63)

CUMMINGS, David
British, born 1937
Holmul. 1970
Acrylic on canvas, 60" x 60"
(152.4 x 152.4 cm)
Acquired 1971
JFKIA (VIP Lounge)

DOWELL, John F.
American
Just a Love Page. 1971
Pen and ink with watercolor, 30" x 22½"
(76.2 x 57.2 cm)
Acquired 1971
WTC

DUBACK, Charles
American, born 1926
E.B.P. 1980. 1980
Charcoal on paper, 50" x 38"
(127 x 96.5 cm)
Acquired 1981
WTC

DURAN, Bob
American, born 1938
Untitled. c. 1971
Acrylic on canvas, 68" x 100"
(172.7 x 254 cm)
Acquired 1971
JFKIA (West Wing, In Transit Lounge,
3d Fl)

EPSTEIN, Beatrice
American
Bird. 1983
Marble, 15" x 2¾" x 5" (38.1 x 7 x 12.7 cm)
Acquired 1984
WTC

ESCHER, Fred
American, born 1940
Neon Sculpture. c. 1970
Assemblage of colored neon tubes,
31" x 23" (78.7 x 58.4 cm)
Acquired 1971
WTC

FEARRINGTON, J. C. Pass
American, 1949–1981
Untitled. 1970
Acrylic on canvas, 63" x 63" (160 x 160 cm)
Acquired 1971
JFKIA (137)

FEINN-PEARSON, Debrah
American, born 1947
Untitled. 1977
Triptych, encaustic on canvas; overall, 72"
x 78" (182.9 x 198.1 cm)
Acquired 1978
WTC

FISH, Janet
American, born 1938
One Bag of Lemons. 1969
Oil on linen, 55" x 56" (139.7 x 142.2 cm)
Acquired 1972
WTC

Two Packages of Pears. 1969
Oil on linen, 52" x 42" (132.1 x 106.7 cm)
Acquired 1972
WTC

Box of Four Apples. 1970
Oil on linen, 30" x 34" (76.2 x 86.4 cm)
Acquired 1971
JFKIA (69)

Two Boxes of Lemons. 1970
Oil on linen, 36" x 48" (91.4 x 121.9 cm)
Acquired 1971
JFKIA (68)

Five Calf's Foot Jelly Jars. 1971
Oil on linen, 30" x 60" (76.2 x 152.4 cm)
Acquired 1972
JFKIA (VIP Lounge)

Windex Bottles. 1971–72
Oil on linen, 50" x 29¾" (127 x 75.6 cm)
Acquired 1972
JFKIA (67)

Vinegar Bottles. 1972
Oil on linen, 50" x 60" (127 x 152.4 cm)
Acquired 1972
JFKIA (66)

FOX, Charles J.
American
Portrait of Austin J. Tobin. 1976
Oil on canvas, 39" x 39" (99.1 x 99.1 cm)
Acquired 1977
WTC
Note: Tobin was the first Executive
Director of the Port Authority

FREI, Linae
American
White Wall. (N.d.)
Three wood panels, each 24" x 24"
(60.9 x 60.9 cm)
Acquired 1972
WTC

FRIEDMAN, Robert
American
Figure. (N.d.)
Aluminum, 32⅝" (82.9 cm) high
Acquired 1976
WTC

GEIST, Del
American, born 1943
Cudjoe, II. 1977
Cor-Ten steel, 44" x 56" x 92"
(111.8 x 142.2 x 233.7 cm)
Acquired 1982
JFKIA

GILCHRIST, William M.
American
Birth of a New Style. 1970
Oil on canvas, 58" x 77" (147.3 x 195.6 cm)
Acquired 1971
JFKIA (65)

GOLDBERG, Helen
American
Portrait of Clifford M. Holland
Oil on canvas, 22" x 18" (55.9 x 45.7 cm)
HT (Administration Building)
Note: Holland was Port Authority Chief
Engineer when the Holland Tunnel
was built.

Untitled (Woman and Sea)
Patinaed-bronze relief, 67" (170.2 cm) high
WTC

GORKY, Arshile (Vosdanig Manoog Adoian)
American, born Turkish Armenia.
1904–1948. To U.S. 1920
*Aviation: Evolution of Forms under
Aerodynamic Limitations: Aerial Map*
1936–37
Oil on canvas, 77" x 10' (195.6 x 307.3 cm)
Commissioned by the WPA Federal Art
Project and installed in second-floor foyer
of Administration Building, Newark
Airport, Newark, New Jersey; painted
over c. 1942; rescued and cleaned 1976
On extended loan to The Newark
Museum, Newark, New Jersey, 1982

Aviation: Evolution of Forms under Aerodynamic Limitations: Mechanics of Flying. 1936–37
Oil on canvas, 108" x 11'1" (271.1 x 328 cm)
Commissioned by the WPA Federal Art Project and installed in second-floor foyer of Administration Building, Newark Airport, Newark, New Jersey; painted over c. 1942; rescued and cleaned 1976
On extended loan to The Newark Museum, Newark, New Jersey, 1982

Modern Aviation. 1981 (after study of 1936–37)
Ceramic mural, after gouache study for panel of *Aviation: Evolution of Forms under Aerodynamic Limitations;* seven parts, overall 96" x 14' (243.8 x 427 cm)
Acquired 1981, gift of Otsuka Chemical Co., Ltd., Osaka, Japan
JFKIA (32)
Note: Gouache study collection Karlen Mooradian, nephew of the artist

GREENBERG, Gloria
American, born 1932
Four Panels. 1971
Acrylic on four canvas panels, each 50" x 50" (127 x 127 cm)
Acquired 1971
JFKIA (22–25)

GRILLO, John
American, born 1917
Bright Farm. 1973
Gouache, 22" x 30" (55.9 x 76.2 cm)
Acquired 1976
WTC

Terrace in Maine. 1973
Gouache, 22" x 30" (55.9 x 76.2 cm)
Acquired 1976
WTC

GUERRERO, José
American, born Spain 1914
Alpujarra. 1963
Oil on canvas, 72" x 72" (182.9 x 182.9 cm)
Acquired 1971
JFKIA

Zoco. 1969
Oil on canvas, 54" x 61" (137.2 x 154.9 cm)
Acquired 1971
JFKIA

HARVEY, James
Canadian, 1929–1965
Cadmium Cobalt Coil. 1964
Oil on canvas, 71" x 71" (180.3 x 180.3 cm)
Acquired 1971
JFKIA (117)

HILL, Clinton J.
American, born 1922
Uneven Sequence. 1967
Oil on canvas, 68" x 55" (172.7 x 139.7 cm)
Acquired 1972
JFKIA (61)

Red Divide. 1971
Oil on canvas, 68" x 55" (172.7 x 139.7 cm)
Acquired 1972
NIA

HO HWAI SHOUH
Chinese, born Canton 1941. In U.S. 1974–76. Lives in Taiwan
Early Spring. 1976
Brush and ink on paper, 27" x 42" (68.6 x 106.7 cm)
Acquired 1977
WTC

A Temporary Refuge. 1976
Brush and ink on paper, 27" x 46" (68.6 x 116.8 cm)
Acquired 1977
WTC

HOKANSON, Hans
American, born Sweden 1925
Helixikos, No. 3. 1969
Bronze (third of eight casts), 39" x 24" x 24" (99.1 x 60.9 x 60.9 cm)
Acquired 1971
JFKIA (35)

Helixikos, No. 18A. 1971
Carved wood, 39" x 24" x 24" (99.1 x 61 x 61 cm); including base, 70" (177.8 cm) high
Acquired 1971
JFKIA (31)

Serpent. 1976
Elm wood, 71" x 24" x 22" (180.3 x 61 x 55.9 cm)
Acquired 1982
JFKIA

HOLMES, Reginald
Canadian, born 1934
Untitled (Blue, Yellow, Green). 1969
Oil on canvas, 46" x 118" (116.8 x 299.7 cm)
Acquired 1971
JFKIA (95)

Untitled (Red, Green, Orange). 1971
Oil on canvas, 42" x 102" (106.7 x 259.1 cm)
Acquired 1971
JFKIA (96)

INUKAI, Kyohei
American, born 1913
Tr@ngloform, IX. c. 1970
Acrylic on canvas, 50" x 60" (127 x 152.4 cm)
Acquired 1971
JFKIA (110)

Triangloform, XI. c. 1970
Acrylic on canvas, 50" x 60" (127 x 152.4 cm)
Acquired 1971
JFKIA (109)

JAPANESE SCHOOL (Zenshu)
View of Daruna. 19th Century
Hanging scroll; brush and ink on paper, 39½" x 9½" (100.3 x 24.1 cm)
Acquired 1970
WTC

JEFFERS, Wendy
American, born 1948
No. 30. 1975
Acrylic and Rhoplex on canvas, 72" x 72" (182.9 x 182.9 cm)
Acquired 1976
WTC

JESSEL, Robert
American, born 1949
Still Life with Apples. c. 1975
Oil on canvas, 32" x 34" (81.3 x 86.4 cm)
Acquired 1976
WTC

Still Life with Teapot. c. 1975
Oil on canvas, 30" x 42" (76.2 x 106.7 cm)
Acquired 1976
WTC

JOHNSON, Lester F.
American, born 1919
Untitled (Black and White). 1970
Ink on paper, 16" x 23" (40.6 x 58.4 cm)
Acquired 1971
WTC

KAUFMAN, Elliott
American, born 1945
Tree Wall No. 1. 1983
Mural on brick facing wall, 45' x 35' (1,371.6 x 1,066.8 cm)
Acquired 1983
HT

KELLER, Germaine
American, born 1938
Study for *PATH Mural.* c. 1978
Ink on paper, two sheets: 29¾" x 42½" (75.6 x 107.9 cm); 28½" x 50" (72.4 x 127 cm)
Acquired 1979
WTC

PATH Mural. 1979
Acrylic on wall, 15" x 75' (38.1 x 2,286 cm)
Acquired 1979
WTC
Note: Created as part of a cooperative program with the Cultural Council Foundation CETA Artists Project, with funds provided by the New York City Department of Employment

KING, Tony
American, born 1944
Triangle. c. 1971
Oil on shaped canvas, each side 60" (152.4 cm)
Acquired 1971
WTC

KNOWLTON, Grace
American, born 1932
Maquette (Proposal for Newark International Airport Sculpture). 1981
Concrete over welded framework reinforced with wire mesh, mounted on board, 4⅜" x 20" x 12¼" (11.1 x 50.8 x 31.1 cm)
Acquired 1981, gift of artist
WTC

KOENIG, Fritz
German, born 1924
Maquette for *Sphere for Plaza Fountain.* 1968
Bronze, 13" (33 cm) high
Acquired 1968
WTC

Sphere for Plaza Fountain. 1969
Bronze (unique cast, 1970–71) on black-granite base, 25' (762 cm) high
Commissioned 1968; installed 1972
WTC (Austin J. Tobin Plaza)

KOSS, Jerzy
American, born Poland 1940. To U.S. 1967
Manhattan Blue. 1974
Acrylic on canvas, 66" x 66" (167.6 x 167.6 cm)
Acquired 1974
WTC (WTI)

LEITES, Susan
American, born 1938
Tulips. 1976
Oil on shaped canvas, 60" x 36" (152.4 x 91.4 cm)
Acquired 1976
WTC (Windows)

Tulips. 1976
Oil on shaped canvas, 60" x 36" (152.4 x 91.4 cm)
Acquired 1976
WTC (Windows)

Crocuses. 1977–79
Oil on shaped canvas, 60" x 36" (152.4 x 91.4 cm)
Acquired c. 1979
WTC (Windows)

Crocuses. 1977–79
Oil on shaped canvas, 60" x 36" (152.4 x 91.4 cm)
Acquired c. 1979
WTC (Windows)

LIEBMANN, Gerhardt
American, born 1928
Bricks. 1969
Acrylic on canvas, 68" x 68" (172.7 cm)
Acquired 1972
WTC

Abyss. 1971
Acrylic on canvas, 86" x 84" (218.4 x 213.4 cm)
Acquired 1972
JFKIA (59)

Approaching Rain. 1971
Acrylic on canvas, 72" x 48" (182.9 x 121.9 cm)
Acquired 1972
WTC

Approaching Storm Front. 1971
Acrylic on canvas, 68" x 68" (172.7 x 172.7 cm)
Acquired 1971
JFKIA (Administration Building)

Sea Shoaling Up to Land. 1971
Acrylic on canvas, 68" x 80" (172.7 x 203.2 cm)
Acquired 1971
JFKIA (Administration Building)

Summer Rain at Sea. 1971
Acrylic on canvas, 86" x 84" (218.4 x 213.4 cm)
Acquired 1971
JFKIA (53)

LINFANTE, Paul
American, born 1940
Apples. 1976
Pastel on paper; two panels, each 40" x 36" (101.6 x 91.4 cm)
Acquired 1976
WTC (Windows)

Wine Bottles. 1976
Pastel on paper, two panels, each 28" x 21" (71.1 x 53.3 cm)
Acquired 1976
WTC (Windows)

LOVING, Alvin
American, born 1935
Diana: Time Trip, II. 1971
Acrylic on canvas, 89" x 20' 8" (226.1 x 630 cm)
Acquired 1972
JFKIA (33)

LUND, David
American, born 1925
Outer Ledge. 1974
Oil on canvas, 36" x 42" (91.4 x 106.7 cm)
Acquired c. 1974
WTC

MACK, Joseph
American, born 1921
Standing Form. 1970
West Indian guango wood, 69" (175.3 cm) high
Acquired 1972
WTC

MACKENZIE, Caroline
American, born 1941
Green. 1969
Acrylic on canvas, 48" x 48" (121.9 x 121.9 cm)
Acquired 1971
JFKIA (21)

MAILMAN, Cynthia
American, born 1942
Maquette for *Commuter Landscape*. 1979
Acrylic on paper mounted on board,
6" x 12" (15.2 x 30.5 cm)
Acquired 1979
WTC

Commuter Landscape. 1979
Acrylic on canvas, 96" x 53' (243.8 x
1,615 cm)
Acquired 1979
PATH (WTC Term)
Note: Created as part of a cooperative
program with Cultural Council
Foundation
CETA Artists Project, with
funds provided by the New York City
Department of Employment.

MALLORY, Ronald
American, born 1935
Cruise Ship Entering New York. 1982
Oil on canvas, 48" x 84" (121.9 x 213.4 cm)
Acquired 1982
WTC (Windows)

MARAVELL, Nicholas
American, born 1955
Swamp Maple. 1981
Oil on panel, 51" x 30" (129.6 x 76.2 cm)
Acquired 1983
WTC

MARTINDALE, James
American, born 1935
No. 14-75. 1975.
Acrylic on shaped canvas panel, 48" x 48"
(121.9 x 121.9 cm)
Acquired 1977
WTC

MEDINA, Rodolfo
Argentine, born 1933
Maquette (Proposal for Port Authority
Bus Terminal Sculpture). 1976
Acrylic on concrete, 34" x 39½" (86.4 x
100.3 cm)
Acquired 1977
WTC

MILLER, Don
American, born Jamaica 1923
Tuareg Grandmother. 1980
Mixed media on canvas, 12" x 14" (30.5 x
35.6 cm)
Acquired 1984
WTC

MIYARUCHI, Haro
Japanese, born 1948
In Canada 1967–70. In U.S. 1970–79
Iris Flower. 1976
Oil over gold ground on canvas, 108" x 48"
(274.3 x 121.9 cm)
Acquired 1976
WTC (Windows)

MOLINARI-FLORES, Luis
Ecuadorian, born 1929. In Argentina
1952–58. In France 1960–65
Construction, No. 28. 1970
Shaped canvas in four parts, each 60" x 12"
x 12" (152.4 x 30.5 x 30.5 cm)
Acquired 1972
JFKIA (20)

After Construction, No. 28 (Yellow). 1970
Acrylic on paper, 30" x 40" (76.2 x
101.6 cm)
Acquired 1971
JFKIA (85)

Gama Amarillo Azul (Range of Yellow Blue).
1970
Acrylic on paper, 30" x 40" (76.2 x
101.6 cm)
Acquired 1971
JFKIA (86)

Salacas. 1970
Acrylic on paper, 30" x 40" (76.2 x
101.6 cm)
Acquired 1971
JFKIA (87)

New York Downtown. 1971
Acrylic on paper, 30" x 40" (76.2 x
101.6 cm)
Acquired 1971
JFKIA (84)

Untitled. 1971
Acrylic on paper, 40" x 30" (101.6 x
76.2 cm)
Acquired 1972
JFKIA (83)

MONROE, Gerald
American, born 1926
Grace Mary. 1973
Oil on canvas, 66" x 60" (167.6 x
152.4 cm)
Acquired 1976
WTC
Note: Also called *Orange, Blue*.

Nancy. 1973
Oil on canvas, 66" x 60" (167.6 x
152.4 cm)
Acquired 1977
WTC

MOULTON, Donn
American, born 1934
Apple. 1973
Enamel on molded fiberglass, 31" x 30"
x 12" (78.7 x 76.2 x 40.5 cm)
Acquired 1973
WTC

Apple. 1973
Enamel on molded fiberglass, 31" x 30"
x 12" (78.7 x 76.2 x 40.5 cm)
Acquired 1973
WTC

MUELLER, Stephen
American, born 1947
Owlhill Club, II. 1970
Oil and acrylic on canvas, 48" x 84" (121.9
x 213.4 cm)
Acquired 1971
JFKIA (70)

NAGARE, Masayuki
Japanese, born 1923
Maquette for *World Trade Center Plaza
Sculpture*. 1969
Black granite, 16¾" x 39¾" (42.5 x
100.9 cm)
Acquired 1969.
WTC

World Trade Center Plaza Sculpture. 1972
Black Swedish granite over concrete and
steel armature, 14' x 34' x 17' (427 x 1,036
x 518 cm); base, 33' 6" long x 15' 9⅞" wide
(1,021 x 482 cm)
Commissioned 1969; installed 1974
WTC (Austin J. Tobin Plaza)

NAUTIYAL, Margaret Reilly
American
Landscape Panorama. 1979
Oil on canvas, 47" x 58" (121.9 x
147.3 cm)
Acquired 1979
WTC

Studio Window, Reflection. 1981
Oil on canvas, 54" x 66" (137.2 x 167.6 cm)
Acquired 1981
WTC

NEVELSON, Louise
American, born Ukraine 1900.
To U.S. 1905
Sky Gate, New York. 1977–78
Black painted wood relief, 17' x 32' x 12"
(518 x 975 x 30.5 cm)
Commissioned 1977; installed 1978
WTC (Tower One, Mezzanine)

NYDORF, Elsie
American
Laughing Dancer
Ceramic sculpture, 32½" x 16" (82.6
x 40.6 cm)
Acquired 1973
WTC

OHLSON, Doug
American, born 1936
Champ, No. 54. 1971
Oil over acrylic on canvas, 66" x 66"
(167.6 x 167.6 cm)
Acquired 1972
JFKIA (136)

OKIMOTO, Jerry
American, born Hawaii 1924
Untitled (No. 70). 1970
Acrylic on canvas, 36" x 108" (91.4
x 274.3 cm)
Acquired 1971
JFKIA (10)

OPPER, John
American, born 1908
No. 16. 1970
Acrylic on canvas, 54" x 66" (137.2
x 167.6 cm)
Acquired 1971
JFKIA (122)

No. 29. 1970
Acrylic on canvas, 55" x 70" (139.7
x 177.8 cm)
Acquired 1971
JFKIA (123)

OVERSTREET, Joe
American, born 1934
Mafia. 1967
Triptych, acrylic on shaped canvas pan-
els; overall, 72" x 87" (182.9 x 221.9 cm)
Acquired 1970
WTC

PADOVANO, Anthony
American, born 1933. In Italy 1960–62
Study for *Spherical Division*. 1969
Pen and ink on paper, 30" x 40" (76.2 x
101.6 cm)
Acquired 1970
WTC

Study for *Spherical Division*. 1969
Pen and ink on paper, 20⅛" x 25¼" (51.1
x 64.1 cm)
Acquired 1970
WTC

Circle 1970 (Maquette for *Spherical
Division*). 1970
Aluminum (one of three casts), 12"
(30.5 cm) diameter
Acquired 1975
WTC

Spherical Division. 1975
Stainless steel, 12' (366 cm) diameter
Acquired 1975 with funds provided in part
by the U.S. Department of Transportation
JSTC (Courtyard)

PENNEY, Jacqueline
American
Gulls, No. 1. c. 1973
Oil and collage on canvas, 48" x 48" (122 x
122 cm)
Acquired 1973
JSTC

PEREZ, J. Esteban
Chilean, born 1930. To U.S. 1965
Constructivist Space Drawing. 1981
Fifteen fired-porcelain enamel panels on
40-gauge steel; 13 panels, each 34" x 34"
x 3" (86.5 x 86.5 x 7.6 cm), end panels each
34" x 48" x 3" (86.4 x 121.9 x 7.6 cm)
Acquired 1981
PABT (North Wing–B Level)

PERRY, James
American, born 1947
Untitled (77-8). 1977
Laminated pine, 61" x 31½" x 8" (154.9 x 80
x 20.3 cm)
Acquired 1982
WTC

Untitled (77-2). 1977
Laminated pine, 65" x 27" x 9" (165.1 x 68.6
x 22.9 cm)
Acquired 1983
PABT

PITTS, Richard
American, born 1940
Near Boysen Road. 1975
Oil on canvas, 48" x 47¾" (121.9 x 121.3 cm)
Acquired 1976
WTC

POWERS, Harry
American, born c. 1929
Construction. 1970
Lucite, 69" (175.3 cm) high
Acquired 1971
WTC (WTI)

QUAYTMAN, Harvey
American, born 1937
Moon Fancy. 1969
Acrylic and dry pigment on canvas, 38"
x 109" (96.5 x 276.9 cm)
Acquired 1971
JFKIA (13)

RAND, Ellen
American
Green Painting. 1972
Oil on canvas, 48" x 36" (121.9 x 91.4 cm)
Acquired 1973
WTC

RAPP, Joseph
American, born 1947
Floating Cube. 1972
Acrylic on shaped canvas, 52" x 59⅞"
(132.1 x 152.1 cm)
Acquired 1973
WTC

Hollow Cube. 1972
Acrylic on shaped canvas, 60" x 60" (152.4
x 152.4 cm)
Acquired 1973
WTC

Painted Sculpture, No. 1. 1972
Acrylic on four canvas panels, each 24"
x 24" (60.9 x 60.9 cm)
Acquired 1973
LGA

Painted Sculpture, No. 2. 1972
Acrylic on four canvas panels, each 24"
x 24" (60.9 x 60.9 cm)
Acquired 1973
WTC

REESE, Ron
American
Untitled. (N.d.)
Oil on canvas, 52" x 83"
(132.1 x 210.8 cm)
Acquired 1976
WTC

RETHI, Lili
American
World Trade Center, New York. 1967–69
Thirteen pencil sketches of WTC con-
struction site, c. 13½″ x 22½″ (34.3 x 57.2
cm) to 14½″ x 23″ (36.8 x 58.4 cm)
Acquired 1970
WTC

RHOADS, George
American, born 1926
42nd Street Ballroom. 1983
Kinetic sculpture, 96″ x 96″ x 96″ (243.2
x 243.2 x 243.2 cm)
Acquired 1983
PABT (North Wing)

ROOS, Gabrielle
American, born Germany
Blue. 1968
Oil on canvas, 48″ x 48″ (121.9 x 121.9 cm)
Acquired 1971
JFKIA (129)

Orange. 1969
Acrylic on canvas, 60″ x 70″ (152.4
x 177.8 cm)
Acquired 1971
JFKIA (14)

Green. 1970
Acrylic on canvas, 40″ x 100″
(101.6 x 254 cm)
Acquired 1971
JFKIA (16)

No. 9. 1971
Acrylic on canvas, 40″ x 80″ (101.6 x
203.2 cm)
Acquired 1972
JFKIA (12)

No. 12. 1971
Acrylic on canvas in two parts: overall
60″ x 10′6″ (152.4 x 320 cm)
Acquired 1972
JFKIA (15)

No. 13. 1971
Acrylic on canvas, 48″ x 90″ (121.9
x 228.6 cm)
Acquired 1972
JFKIA (11)

Diagonal Orange, No. 1. 1972
Acrylic on canvas, 54″ x 72″ (137.2
x 182.9 cm)
Acquired 1975
WTC

Diagonal Red, No. 1. 1972
Acrylic on canvas, 54″ x 72″ (137.2
x 182.9 cm)
Acquired 1975
WTC

ROSATI, James
American, born 1912
Ideogram. 1974
Stainless steel, 23′6″ x 19′6″ x 28′6″
(816.7 x 594.6 x 974.3 cm)
Commissioned 1969; installed 1974
WTC (Austin J. Tobin Plaza)
Note: Fabricated after zinc maquette
(1967), 23¼″ x 19½″ x 28½″, collection the
artist

ROTH, Richard
American, born 1927
Moop, No. 12. 1974
Acrylic on canvas, 46″ x 62″ (116.8
x 157.5 cm)
Acquired 1975
WTC

RUBAN, James
American, born 1928. In Cuba and Mexico
1949–51
Big Diamond. 1970
Acrylic on two canvas panels, each 64″
x 64″ (162.6 x 162.6 cm)
Acquired 1977
WTC

RUDA, Edwin
American, born 1922
Chief Kisco. 1970
Acrylic on canvas, 70″ x 90″ (177.8 x
228.6 cm)
Acquired 1971
JFKIA (71)

SALT, John
British, born 1937
Skylark. 1969
Oil on canvas, 53″ x 69″ (134.6 x 175.3 cm)
Acquired 1972
JFKIA (60)

SAMALIN, Alan
American, born 1945
Picturing Flight. 1982
Acrylic on canvas, 62″ x 121′6″ (157.5 x
3,703.3 cm)
Acquired 1982, created as part of a cooper-
ative program with the Cultural Council
Foundation CETA Artists Project, with
funds provided by the New York City
Department of Employment.
JFKIA (Control Tower Lobby)

SAMSON, Lancelot
Dutch, born 1938
Union. 1981
Carrara marble, 90″ x 20″ (228.6 x 50.8 cm)
Acquired 1982, gift from city of
Rotterdam
WTC (Observation Deck)

SANGUINO, Luis Antonio
Spanish, born 1934. In U.S. 1957–72
Bust of Fiorello H. LaGuardia. 1964
Marble, 9′ (274.3 cm) high
Acquired 1964
LAG (Central Term Bldg, 2d Fl Lobby)
Note: LaGuardia, Mayor of New York
1934-45, was responsible for building
LaGuardia Airport, 1939. Bust installed
on occasion of completion of new termi-
nal, 1964

Bust of Fiorello H. LaGuardia. 1964
Bronze, c. 9″ (22.9 cm) high
Acquired 1964
LAG (Hangar 7, Conf Rm)

SANJUL, Margot
Guatemalan
Dark Green. 1966
Acrylic on canvas, 63″ x 81″ (160 x
205.1 cm)
On loan from Center for Inter-American
Relations, New York
WTC

Orange Crush, No. 2
Acrylic on shaped canvas, 79″ (200.7 cm)
diameter
On loan from Center for Inter-American
Relations, New York
JSTC

Pink and Red
Acrylic on canvas, 81″ x 63″ (205.7 x
160 cm)
On loan from Center for Inter-American
Relations, New York
WTC

SAWANO, Mizue
Japanese, born 1941
Lily Pond, I: Autumn after the Storm. 1980
Oil on linen, 50″ x 60″ (127 x 152.4 cm)
Acquired 1981
WTC (Windows)

Lily Pond, II: Summer Life. 1980
Oil on linen, 50″ x 60″ (127 x 152.4 cm)
Acquired 1981
WTC (Windows)

SCHILLING, Alfons
Swiss, born 1934
Washington, II. 1969–70
Photoemulsion on lenticular, transparent-
plastic screen, 67¾″ x 59¼″ (172.1 x
150.5 cm)
Acquired 1971
JFKIA (54)

SEGAL, George
American, born 1924
The Commuters. 1980
Bronze with white patina (cast 1981), 84″
x 72″ x 96″ (213.4 x 182.9 x 243.8 cm)
Commissioned 1979; installed 1982
PABT (South Wing)

SENUFO TRIBE (Dahomey)
Masked Figure
Wood, 36″ (91.4 cm) high
Acquired 1973
WTC

SHEDDEN, Charles
American
Lovers Never Say Goodbye. c. 1971
Fiberglass, 31″ (78.7 cm) high x 72″
(182.9 cm) in circumference
Acquired 1971
WTC

SHORE, Richard
American, 1943–1982
Maquette for *Slice.* 1973
Cor-Ten Steel, 8″ x 14″ (20.3 x 35.6 cm)
Acquired 1977
WTC

Slice. 1975
Cor-Ten steel, 96″ x 14′ (243.8 x 427 cm)
Commissioned 1975; installed 1977
NIA (Administration Building Courtyard)

SINDORF, Robert Johannes, Jr.
American, born the Netherlands 1951
Times Past. 1981
Italian white marble, 36″ x 18″ x 4″ (91.4 x
45.7 x 10.1 cm); including base, 74″
(187.9 cm) high
Acquired 1982
JFKIA

SLIVKA, David.
American, born 1914
Untitled. August 11, 1964.
Brush and ink on paper, 40″ x 26″ (101.6 x
66 cm)
Acquired 1971
JFKIA (55)

Untitled. August 14, 1964
Brush and ink on paper, 40″ x 26½″ (101.6
x 67.3 cm)
Acquired 1970
WTC

Figure. 1970
Brush and ink on paper, 30″ x 22″ (76.2
x 55.9 cm)
Acquired 1970
WTC

Phoenix. May 1970
Brush and ink on paper, 40″ x 26″ (101.6
x 66 cm)
Acquired 1971
JFKIA (58)

Blue Landscape, No. 3. September 20, 1970
Brush and ink on paper, 22½″ x 30⅜″ (55.9
x 77.4 cm)
Acquired 1970
WTC

Untitled. 1970
Brush and ink on paper, 22¼″ x 26⅝″ (56.5
x 67.6 cm)
Acquired 1970
WTC

Juggernaut, I. April 17, 1971
Brush and ink on paper, 26″ x 40″ (66
x 101.6 cm)
Acquired 1971
JFKIA (57)

Brahmin. April 25, 1971
Brush and ink on paper, 38″ x 24½″ (96.5
x 62.2 cm)
Acquired 1971
JFKIA (56)

Recuerdo, I (Remembrance). June 1, 1971
Brush and ink on paper, 38″ x 50″ (96.5
x 127 cm)
Acquired 1971
JFKIA (5)

Habitat, I. June 2, 1971
Brush and ink on paper, 38″ x 49″ (96.5
x 124.5 cm)
Acquired 1971
JFKIA (4)

Machu Picchu, IV. October 5, 1971
Brush and ink on paper, 50″ x 38″ (127
x 96.5 cm)
Acquired 1972
JFKIA (3)

Machu Picchu, V. October 6, 1971
Brush and ink on paper, 50″ x 38″ (127 x
96.5 cm)
Acquired 1972
JFKIA (2)

Machu Picchu, VI. October 7, 1971
Brush and ink on paper, 50″ x 38″ (127 x
96.5 cm)
Acquired 1972
JFKIA (1)

Dark Reach. 1971
Ink and acrylic on posterboard, 38″ x 50″
(96.5 x 127 cm)
Acquired 1972
WTC

Germinal. 1971
Ink and acrylic on posterboard, 50″ x 38″
(127 x 96.5 cm)
Acquired 1972
WTC

Gulliver. 1971
Ink and acrylic on posterboard, 50″ x 38″
(127 x 96.5 cm)
Acquired 1972
WTC

SLONEM, Hunt
American, born 1951
Study for *Fan Dancing with the Birds.* 1978
Oil-base enamel and varnish on paper,
4½″ x 10½″ (11.4 x 26.7 cm)
Acquired 1978
WTC

Fan Dancing with the Birds. 1978
Mural; oil-base enamel and varnish on
wall, 96″ x 45′ (243.8 x 1,372 cm)
Acquired 1978
WTC
Note: Created as part of a cooperative
program with Cultural Council
Foundation CETA Artists Project, with
funds provided by the New York City
Department of Employment

SMERECHNIAK, Ron
American, born 1933
Nos. 1 and 2. 1970
Acrylic on two canvas panels, each 76"
x 76" (193 x 193 cm)
Acquired 1971
JFKIA (127, 128)

SNELSON, Kenneth
American, born 1927
Needle Tower. 1968
Aluminum and stainless steel wire, 96"
(243.8 cm) high
Acquired 1981
WTC (Windows)

STALLER, Eric
American, born 1947
N.Y.U.F.O. 1983
Sheet metal with incandescent light
bulbs, 10' x 10' x 10' (304 x 304 x 304 cm)
Installed 1983
PABT (South Wing)
Note: Leased from artist for five years; on
view three months a year

Slither. 1983
Sheet metal and incandescent light bulbs
with light sequencer, 30' x 30' (912
x 912 cm)
Installed 1983
PABT (North Wing)
Note: Leased from artist for five years; on
view three months a year

STERN, Marina
American, born Italy 1928. To U.S. 1941
George Washington Bridge, Nos. 1 and 2.
1971
Oil on two canvas panels, each 58" x 36"
(147.3 x 91.4 cm)
Acquired 1971
WTC

SUGAI, Kumi
Japanese, born 1921. To Paris 1952
Untitled. 1970. Published by Librairie-
Galerie La Hune, Paris
Nickled brass (128 of 150),
9" (22.9 cm) high
Acquired 1970
WTC

TAGGART, Terry
American
CN 1677. 1970
Acrylic on canvas, 67" x 107" (170.2
x 271.8 cm)
Acquired 1971
JFKIA (64)

TAGGART, William
American, born 1940
Jonah. 1971
Fiberglass and wood, 75" x 90" x 84"
(190.5 x 228.6 x 213.4 cm)
Acquired 1972
JFKIA (124)

TOYOSHIMA, Soroku
Japanese, born 1939. Lives in U.S.
No. 16. 1968
Aluminum and iron (unique cast), 84"
x 51" x 34" (213.3 x 129.6 x 86.3 cm)
Acquired 1971
JFKIA (106)

VALLILA, Marja
American, born 1950
Elevated Plaza. 1980
Steel and copper, 54" x 38" x 20" (137.2
x 96.5 x 50.8 cm)
Acquired 1982
JFKIA

VASA (Velizar Mihich)
American, born Yugoslavia 1933
BA-3. 1972
Plexiglass; three columns, each 11" x 4½"
x 2½" (27.9 x 11.4 x 6.4 cm)
Acquired 1973
WTC

BA-12. 1972
Plexiglass; four columns, each 23½" x 3"
x 2" (59.7 x 7.6 x 5.1 cm)
Acquired 1973
WTC

VON ROTH, Frederick G.
George Washington
Bronze, 35" (88.9 cm) high
Acquired 1967
GWB Bus Station Concourse

WEBER, Willy
Swiss, born 1933
Space Dream. 1971
Stainless steel, 54" x 59" (137.2 x 149.9 cm)
Acquired 1972
JFKIA (126)

WERNER, Fred
American, born 1938
Wine Grapes. 1976
Oil on canvas, 60" x 48" (152.4 x 121.9 cm)
Acquired 1976
WTC

Astronomical: A Triptych. 1977
Oil and collage on three canvas panels;
overall, 60" x 10' (152.4 x 304.8 cm)
Acquired 1977
WTC (Windows)

Ocean. 1978
Oil on canvas, 96" x 60" (243.8 x 152.4 cm)
Acquired 1978
WTC (Windows)

WILDER, Joseph
American, born 1920
Graham Hill at Watkins Glen. 1971
Oil on canvas, 72" x 48" (182.9 x 121.9 cm)
Acquired 1972
JFKIA (26)

WILLIAMS, Wheeler
American, 1897–1972
Bust of Clifford M. Holland. (N.d.)
Bronze, 28" (71.1 cm) high
Commissioned 1953 for twenty-fifth
anniversary of Holland Tunnel
HT (NY Portal)
Note: Holland was Port Authority Chief
Engineer when the Holland Tunnel was
built.

Bust of O. H. Ammann. 1965
Bronze, 27½" (69.9 cm) high
Commissioned 1962; dedicated Fall 1965
at the opening of the lower level of George
Washington Bridge
GWB Bus Station Concourse
Note: Othmar H. Ammann is the engineer
who designed the George Washington
Bridge

WISSEMANN-WIDRIG, Nancy
American, born 1930
Director's Chair. 1971
Acrylic on canvas, 42" x 50" (106.7
x 127 cm)
Acquired 1973
WTC

WOJCIK, Gary
American, born 1945
Column. 1970
Painted steel, 60" (152.4 cm) high
Acquired 1971
JFKIA (34)

YOST, Erma Martin
American, born 1947
Blue Horizon. 1974
Oil and modeling paste on canvas, 31"
x 61" (78.7 x 154.9 cm)
Acquired 1977
WTC

Purple Palisades. 1974
Oil and modeling paste on canvas, 41"
x 53" (104.1 x 134.6 cm)
Acquired 1977
WTC

YUCIKAS, Robert
American, born 1944
La Ciotat. 1970
Acrylic on canvas, 62" x 61" (157.5
x 154.9 cm)
Acquired 1971
JFKIA (97)

Eve, II. 1970
Acrylic on canvas, 62" x 61" (157.5
x 154.9 cm)
Acquired 1971
JFKIA (98)

Len. 1970
Acrylic on canvas, 62" x 61" (157.5
x 154.9 cm)
Acquired 1971
JFKIA (Administration Building)

ZEHNER, Earl
American, born 1935
Turbulence in the Bay. 1968
Oil on canvas, 36" x 50½" (91.4 x 128.3 cm)
Acquired 1970
WTC

Prints and Posters

ADAMI, Valerio
Italian, born 1935
Untitled plate from *El Circulo de Piedra
(Circle of Stone).* 1969. Grafica Uno, Milan
Lithograph, 17¾" x 22¼" (45.1 x 56.5 cm)
Acquired 1970
JFKIA (44)
Note: Portfolio of 15 plates with Spanish
text by Carlos Franqui, published in an
edition of 125

AKIRA
American, born Hawaii 1950. To mainland
U.S. 1975
Untitled, Nos. 1-4, from *Rock Paper Scis-
sors.* 1978
Four silkscreen prints with mixed media
on posterboard, each in an edition of four;
each 49" x 31" (124.5 x 78.7 cm); image, 44"
x 28" (111.8 x 71.1 cm)
Commissioned by the PATH Corporation
through the Cultural Council Foundation
CETA Artists Project, 1978
WTC
Note: *Rock Paper Scissors,* containing title
poster and four silkscreens by each of 12
artists, was created for installation at
PATH Ninth Street Station off Sixth Avenue, New York, August 1979–June 1980

ALECHINSKY, Pierre
Belgian, born 1927. Lives in France
Tout à Trac (All of a Sudden). 1971. Li-
brairie-Galerie La Hune, Paris
Color lithograph (62/100), 30" x 16¾" (76.5
x 42.5 cm)
Acquired 1971
NIA

Les 12 Coups de Midi (Twelve Noon).
Lithograph (100/100), 30" x 21¾" (76.2 x
55.2 cm)
Acquired 1971
WTC

ALTMAN, Harold
American, born 1924
Children, Parc Monceau. 1982
Lithograph (148/185), 21" x 30" (53.3 x
76.2 cm)
Acquired 1984
JSTC

Bridle Path. 1984
Lithograph (14/285), 30" x 21" (76.2 x
53.3 cm)
Acquired 1984
JSTC

ANUSZKIEWICZ, Richard J.
American, born 1930
Plates 1–10 from *Sequential.* 1972. Pace
Editions, New York
Serigraph (137/200), each 28⅛" x 21½"
(71.4 x 54.6 cm)
Acquired 1973
JFKIA (99)

Vote for New York. 1968
Silkscreen poster (119/144), 35½" x 25½"
(90.2 x 64.8 cm)
WTC

Vote for New York. 1968
Silkscreen poster from an edition of 144,
35½" x 25½" (90.2 x 64.8 cm)
Acquired 1971
WTC

APPEL, Karel
Dutch, born 1921. To Paris 1950. Lives in
U.S.
Dancing in the Spring. 1970
Serigraph (100/100), 28½" x 41¼" (71.8 x
104.8 cm)
Acquired 1971
JFKIA (114)

Dream-Colored Head. 1970
Serigraph (90/100), 28¼" x 41¼" (71.8 x
140.8 cm)
Acquired 1971
JFKIA (113)

Looking to the Infinite. 1970
Serigraph (94/100), 28¼" x 41¼" (71.8 x
104.8 cm)
Acquired 1971
JFKIA (115)

Walking Alone. 1970
Serigraph (100/100), 41¼" x 28¼" (104.8 x
71.8 cm)
Acquired 1971
JFKIA (116)

Yellow Face. 1971
Color serigraph (99/100), 26" x 19⅝" (66 x
50 cm)
Acquired 1971
WTC

AUSBY, Ellsworth
American, born 1942
Space Odyssey, Nos. 1–4, from *Rock Paper
Scissors.* 1978
Four silkscreen prints with mixed media
on posterboard, each in an edition of four;
each 31" x 49" (78.7 x 124.5 cm); 28" x 44"
(71.1 x 111.8 cm), image
Commissioned by the PATH Corporation
through the Cultural Council Foundation
CETA Artists Projects, 1978
WTC
Note: See AKIRA

BANERJEE, Bimal
American, born India 1939
Homage to New York with Love, Nos. 1–4,
from *Rock Paper Scissors*. 1978
Four silkscreen prints on posterboard,
each in an edition of four; each 31″ x 49″
(124.5 x 78.7 cm); 28″ x 44″ (71.1 x
111.8 cm), image.
Commissioned by the PATH Corporation
through the Cultural Council Foundation
CETA Artists Project, 1978
WTC
Note: See AKIRA

BASKIN, Leonard
American, born 1922
Fuseli. 1969. Lublin Graphics, Greenwich,
Connecticut
Lithograph (1/100), 13¾″ x 20½″ (34.9 x
52.1 cm), image
Acquired 1970
WTC

Monticelli. 1969. Lublin Graphics, Greenwich, Connecticut
Etching (73/100), 32½″ x 31½″ (82.6 x
80 cm)
Acquired 1971
WTC
Note: Adolphe Joseph Thomas Monticelli
(1824–1886) was a French landscape,
genre, and portrait painter

Watteau. 1969
Etching (8/70), 26¾″ x 29¾″ (67.9 x
75.6 cm)
Acquired 1970
WTC
Note: Jean Antoine Watteau (1684–1721)
was the French painter

BATLLE, Georgette
American, born 1942
New York Profiles. 1974
Twelve silkscreen prints, each 45″ x 30″
(114.3 x 76.2 cm)
Acquired 1983
PABT

BUFFET, Bernard
French, born 1928
Bullfighters
Color lithograph (63/150), 29″ x 20″ (73.7 x
50.8 cm), image
Acquired 1970
WTC

Les Fleurs (Flowers)
Color lithograph (64/125), 23½″ x 18½″
(59.7 x 47 cm)
Acquired 1971
WTC

Matador
Color lithograph (63/150), 29″, x 20″ (73.7 x
50.8 cm), image
Acquired 1970
WTC

Le Mélancolique (Melancholy One)
Color lithograph, 33½″ x 27¾″ (85.1 x
70.5 cm)
Acquired 1971
JFKIA (Control Tower, 3d Fl)

New York
Color lithograph (15/150), 29″ x 21½″ (73.7 x
54.6 cm)
Acquired 1969
WTC

New York
Color lithograph (138/150), 29″ x 21½″
(73.7 x 54.6 cm)
Acquired 1971
WTC

CALDER, Alexander
American, 1898–1976. Lived in France
and U.S.
African Figures
Lithograph (142/150), 29⅝″ x 23¾″ (75.2 x
60.3 cm)
Acquired 1971
WTC

Bubbles d'Air (Air Bubbles). 1969. Galerie
Maeght, Paris
Lithograph from an edition of 75, 30½″ x
22⅞″ (77.4 x 58.1 cm)
Acquired 1970
WTC

Circles
Lithograph (10/115), 21⅞″ x 30⅞″ (55.6 x
78.4 cm)
Acquired 1971
WTC

Circles
Color lithograph (49/75), 43¼″ x 29¼″
(109.9 x 74.3 cm)
Acquired 1971
JFKIA (104)

Composition. Lublin Graphics,
Greenwich, Connecticut
Lithograph from an edition of 130,
21″ x 28″ (53.3 x 71.1 cm)
Acquired 1969
JSTC

*Couleurs Enlacées dans le Fil de Fer (Colors
Entwined in Wire)*
Lithograph, 29½″ x 43¼″ (74.9 x 109.9 cm)
Acquired 1971
JFKIA (103)

Far West. 1967. Galerie Maeght, Paris
Color lithograph (55/90), 43½″ x 30″ (110.5
x 76.2 cm)
Acquired 1971
JFKIA (52)

Phrygien et Fer (Phrygian with Sword). 1969
Color lithograph (67/75), 29¼″ x 43¼″
(74.3 x 109.9 cm)
Acquired 1971
JFKIA (102)

Spirales (Spirals)
Lithograph, 29½″ x 20″ (74.9 x 50.8 cm)
Acquired 1971
WTC

The Sun
Lithograph (19/100), 25⅞″ x 35½″ (65.7 x
90.2 cm)
Acquired 1970
WTC

Untitled plate from *El Circulo de Piedra
(Circle of Stone)*. 1969. Grafica Uno, Milan
Lithograph, 22¼″ x 17¾″ (56.5 x 45.1 cm)
Acquired 1970
JFKIA (49)
Note: See ADAMI

CAMACHO, Jorge
Cuban, born 1934. To France c. 1964
Untitled plate from *El Circulo de Piedra
(Circle of Stone)*. 1969. Grafica Uno, Milan
Lithograph, 22¼″ x 17¾″ (56.5 x 45.1 cm)
Acquired 1970
JFKIA (47)
Note: See ADAMI

CARDENAS, Agustin
Cuban, born 1927. To France 1959
Untitled plate from *El Circulo de Piedra
(Circle of Stone)*. 1969. Grafica Uno, Milan
Lithograph, 22¼″ x 17¾″ (56.5 x 45.1 cm)
Acquired 1970
JFKIA (38)
Note: See ADAMI

CARVIN, Robert
American, born 1952
Paint Stands Up, Nos. 1–4, from *Rock Paper
Scissors*. 1978
Four silkscreen prints with mixed media
on posterboard, each in an edition of four;
two, 49″ x 31″ (124.5 x 78.7 cm) two, 31″ x
49″; 44″ x 28″ (111.8 x 71.1 cm), and 28″ x
44″, image
Commissioned by the PATH Corporation
through the Cultural Council Foundation
CETA Artists Project, 1978
WTC
Note: See AKIRA

CESAR (César Baldaccini)
French, born 1921
Untitled plate from *El Circulo de Piedra
(Circle of Stone)*. 1969. Grafica Uno, Milan
Lithograph, 17¾″ x 22¼″ (45.1 x 56.5 cm)
Acquired 1970
JFKIA (37)
Note: See ADAMI

CHERMAYEFF, Ivan
American, born England 1932
Black Relationship. 1970. Pace Editions,
New York
Lithograph (21/100), 29¼″ x 25½″ (74.3 x
64.8 cm)
Acquired 1971
WTC

Blue and Green. 1970. Pace Editions, New
York
Lithograph (21/100), 29¼″ x 25½″ (74.3 x
64.8 cm)
Acquired 1971
WTC

CHERRY, Herman
American, born 1909
Untitled, Nos. 1–4, from *Rock Paper
Scissors*. 1978
Four silkscreen prints with mixed media
on posterboard, each in an edition of four;
each 49″ x 31″ (124.5 x 78.7 cm); 44″ x 28″
(111.8 x 71.1 cm), image
Commissioned by the PATH Corporation
through the Cultural Council Foundation
CETA Artists Project, 1978
WTC
Note: See AKIRA

CLARKE, John Clem
American, born 1937
Chardin: "The Bubble Blower." 1970
Brooke Alexander, New York
Lithograph (69/90), 31″ x 23″
(89.7 x 58.4 cm)
Acquired 1971
WTC

CLERK, Pierre
American, born 1928. In Canada 1932–52.
In France 1952–54. In Italy 1954–59. To
U.S. 1959.
Black and White. 1970
Serigraph (27/50), 41″ x 33″ (104 x 83.8 cm)
Acquired 1971
JFKIA (135)

Black and White. 1970
Serigraph (37/50), 41″ x 33″ (104 x 83.8 cm)
Acquired 1971
JFKIA (134)

Tension Series: Black and White. 1971
Serigraph (55/75), 41″ x 33″ (104 x 83.8 cm)
Acquired 1971
JFKIA (131)

Tension Series: Red, Black, Yellow. 1971
Serigraph (56/75), 41″ x 33″ (104 x 83.8 cm)
Acquired 1971
JFKIA (132)

Tension Series: Red, Blue, Yellow. 1971
Serigraph (54/75), 41″ x 33″ (104 x 83.8 cm)
Acquired 1971
JFKIA (130)

Tension Series: Red, White, Blue. 1971
Serigraph (54/75), 41″ x 33″ (104 x 83.8 cm)
Acquired 1971
JFKIA (133)

CORNEILLE (Cornelius Guillaume van
Beverloo)
Dutch, born Belgium 1922.
To Paris 1950
Untitled plate from *El Circulo de Piedra
(Circle of Stone)*. 1969.
Lithograph, 22¼″ x 17¾″ (56.5 x 45.1 cm)
Acquired 1970
JFKIA (41)
Note: See ADAMI

CUEVAS, José Luis
Mexican, born 1934. In U.S. 1957, 1970,
1975
*Lo Feo de Este Mundo, I (The Ugliness of
This World)* from *Homage to Quevedo*.
1969. Collector's Press, San Francisco
Color lithograph (19/100) from portfolio of
14 plates, 22″ x 30″ (55.9 x 76.2 cm)
Acquired 1971
JFKIA (28)
Note: Quevedo (1580–1645) was the
Spanish writer.

La Mascara (The Mask) from *Homage to
Quevedo*. 1969
Collector's Press, San Francisco
Embossed lithograph with gold acetate
(24/100) from portfolio of 14 plates,
30″ x 22″ (76.2 x 55.9 cm)
Acquired 1970
JFKIA (27)

El Santo de la Guerra (Patron Saint of War)
from *Homage to Quevedo*. 1969
Collector's Press, San Francisco
Color lithograph (2/100) from portfolio of
14 plates, 30″ x 22″ (76.2 x 55.9 cm)
Acquired 1971
JFKIA (29)

El Viaje (The Journey) from *Homage to
Quevedo*. 1969.
Collector's Press, San Francisco
Color lithograph (2/100) from portfolio of
14 plates, 30″ x 22″ (76.2 x 55.9 cm)
Acquired 1971
WTC

DALI, Salvador
Spanish, born 1904.
Lives in France
Jousting. 1962
Color etching, 13¾″ x 21″ (34.9 x 53.3 cm)
Acquired 1971
WTC

Coeur (Heart). 1967. C.F.A. Graphics,
New York
Etching (56/200), 22″ x 20″ (55.9 x 50.8 cm)
Acquired 1971
WTC

Don Quixote. 1970
Drypoint on Japon nacré paper (55/175),
30″ x 22″ (76 x 56 cm)
Acquired 1970
WTC

Sancho Panza. 1970
Drypoint on Japon nacré paper (25/175),
30″ x 22″ (76 x 56 cm)
Acquired 1971
WTC

Sancho Panza. 1970
Drypoint on Japon nacré paper (51/175),
30″ x 22″ (76 x 56 cm)
Acquired 1970
WTC

Famous People Series: Edison
Etching (68/125), 12½″ x 16″
(31.8 x 40.6 cm)
Acquired 1970
WTC

Famous People Series: Einstein
Etching (51/150), 12½" x 16" (31.8 x
40.6 cm)
Acquired 1970
NIA (Administration Building)

Famous People Series: van Gogh
Etching (43/150), 12½" x 16"
(31.8 x 40.6 cm)
Acquired 1970
WTC

John Kennedy
Etching (59/60), 16" x 13½" (40.6 x 34.3 cm)
Acquired 1970
WTC

La Lune (Moon). 1970. C.F.A. Graphics,
New York
Etching (37/200), 30" x 22" (76.2 x 55.9 cm)
Acquired 1971
WTC

El Vigne (The Vineyard)
Etching, 31" x 23" (78.7 x 58.4 cm)
Acquired 1970
WTC

Memories of Surrealism. 1971
Portfolio of 12 plates and four text pages
(28/175), lithography, etching, and photo-
engraving, each 30" x 21¼" (75 x 53 cm)
Acquired 1971
JFKIA
Note: Etched by Atelier Risal, Fontenay-
aux-Roses, France. Lithographed by
Claude Jobin, Paris.

D'ARCANGELO, Allan
American, born 1930
Composition
Lithograph (54/100), 39¼" x 24¼"
(76.8 x 61.6)
Acquired 1971
WTC

Road Series. 1966. Hollanders Workshop,
New York
Lithograph (15/25), 21¼" x 21½"
(53.3 x 54.3 cm)
Acquired 1970
WTC

Lincoln Center Festival. 1968
H.K.L. Ltd., Boston
Silkscreen poster (82/144), 45" x 29¼"
(114.3 x 74.3 cm)
Acquired 1971
JFKIA (82)

National Collection of Fine Arts. 1968
Silkscreen poster, 45" x 29⅛"
(114.3 x 74 cm)
JFKIA (81)

DELAUNAY, Sonia
French, born Ukraine. 1885–1979
Blue, Green, Black, Red, Gray, White
Aquatint (86/100) 29¾" x 21¼"
(75.6 x 54 cm)
Acquired 1970
WTC

Plates 1–6 from *Six Lithographs*. 1961
Color lithographs, each 28" x 20"
(71 x 51 cm)
Acquired 1970
WTC

Untitled
Serigraph (103/150), 29¾" x 22"
(75.6 x 55.9 cm)
Acquired 1972
WTC

Venise (Venice). 1969
Color lithograph (25/75), 25½" x 19⅝"
(65 x 50 cm)
Acquired 1970
WTC

Venise (Venice). 1969
Color lithograph (73/75), 25½" x 19⅝"
(65 x 50 cm)
Acquired 1970
NIA (Administration Building)

Contrastes (Contrasts). 1970. Librairie-
Galerie La Hune, Paris
Serigraph (44/75), 24" x 30½"
(60.9 x 77.5 cm)
Acquired 1971
WTC

Les Soleils (Suns). 1970.
Color lithograph (64/75), 30" x 22"
(76 x 56 cm)
Acquired 1970
WTC

DEWASNE, Jean
French, born 1921
Plates 1–14 from *Progression*. 1969
Serigraph, each 29" x 19" (73.7 x 48.3 cm)
Acquired 1971
JFKIA (100)

DIEBENKORN, Richard
American, born 1922
Untitled plate from *Ten West Coast Artists*.
1965
Collector's Press, San Francisco
Lithograph (17/75), 30" x 22"
(76.2 x 55.9 cm)
Acquired 1970
WTC

ERRO (Gudmundur Gudmundsson)
Icelandic, born 1932. Lives in Paris
Untitled plate from *El Circulo de Piedra
(Circle of Stone)*. 1969. Grafica Uno, Milan
Lithograph, 17¾" x 22¼" (45.1 x 56.5 cm)
Acquired 1970
JFKIA (51)
Note: See ADAMI

FRANCIS, Sam (Samuel Lewis)
American born 1923. In France 1950–60
Three Images. 1967. Hollanders Workshop,
New York
Lithograph (T.P.), 22" x 30" (55.9 x 76.2 cm)
Acquired 1970
WTC

Untitled plate from *Portfolio 9*. 1967.
Hollanders Workshop, New York
Color lithograph (66/100), 17" x 22"
(43.2 x 55.9 cm)
Acquired 1970
WTC
Note: Portfolio published in collaboration
with the Whitney Museum of American
Art, New York. Consists of one plate each
by nine artists: Francis, Ellsworth Kelly,
Willem de Koonig, Roy Lichtenstein,
Richard Lindner, Robert Motherwell,
Louise Nevelson, Henry Pearson, and Saul
Steinberg

FRIEDLAENDER, Johnny
German, born 1912
En Mesure (On Time). 1966
Color etching (54/95), 39" x 32½"
(99 x 82.6 cm)
Acquired 1970
WTC

Fastes (Records). 1968
Color etching (6/85), 30⅜" x 22½"
(77.2 x 57 cm)
Acquired 1970
WTC

Herbes Solaires (Solar Grass). 1969
Color etching (65/95), 30" x 22¼"
(76 x 56.5 cm)
Acquired 1971
WTC

Oiseau Brun (Brown Bird). 1969
Color etching (76/95), 29½" x 21½"
(75 x 57.2 cm)
Acquired 1970
WTC

*Oiseau et Son Ombre (Bird and Its
Shadow)*. 1969
Etching (13/95), 29⅞" x 22¼"
(75.9 x 56.5 cm)
Acquired 1971
Truck Terminal (325 Spring Street)

Passacaille (Passacaglia). 1969
Color etching (7/95), 30" x 22½"
(76.5 x 57.2 cm)
Acquired 1970
WTC

Passacaille (Passacaglia). 1969
Color etching (18/95), 30" x 22½"
(76.5 x 57.2 cm)
Acquired 1970
WTC

Soleil d'Hiver (Winter Sun). 1969
Color etching (56/95), 22⅛" x 30"
(56.3 x 76.5 cm)
Acquired 1969
WTC

Symbole (Symbol). 1969. Librairie-Galerie
La Hune, Paris
Color etching (2/95), 30" x 22"
(76.5 x 55.9 cm)
Acquired 1971
Port Newark

Oiseau dans le Cercle (Bird in the Circle).
1970
Color etching (A.P.), 30" x 22"
(76.5 x 55.9 cm)
Acquired 1971
WTC

Oiseau dans le Cercle (Bird in the Circle).
1970
Color etching (A.P.), 30" x 22"
(76.5 x 55.9 cm)
Acquired 1971
WTC

Première Conclusion (First Conclusion).
1970
Color etching (A.P.), 30" x 22¼"
(76.5 x 56.5 cm)
Acquired 1970
WTC

Trilogie (Trilogy). 1970
Color etching (63/95), 30" x 22½"
(76.5 x 56.5 cm)
Acquired 1970
WTC

*Vers le Nord et vers le Sud
(Northbound and Southbound)*. 1970
Color etching (6/85), 30¼" x 22¼"
(77.2 x 56.7 cm)
Acquired 1970
WTC

*Vers le Nord et vers le Sud
(Northbound and Southbound)*. 1970
Color etching (12/95), 30¼" x 22¼"
(77.2 x 56.7 cm)
Acquired 1971
WTC

Untitled.
Color etching (5/95), 30" x 22¼"
(76.2 x 56.5 cm)
Acquired 1971
WTC

Accord Vert (Green Accord). 1972
Color etching (59/94), 30" x 22½"
(65.2 x 57.2 cm)
Acquired 1978
WTC

GOLOB, Stanford
American, born 1947
Waterside, Nos. 1–4, from
Rock Paper Scissors. 1978
Four silkscreen prints with mixed media
on posterboard, each in an edition of four;
each 49" x 31" (124.5 x 78.7 cm); 44" x 28"
(111.8 x 71 cm), image
Commissioned by the PATH Corporation
through the Cultural Council Foundation
CETA Artists Project, 1978
WTC
Note: See AKIRA

GRUEN, John
American, born 1938
*Whiskbroom with Five Supporting
Objects*, Nos. 1–4, from *Rock Paper
Scissors*. 1978
Four silkscreen prints with mixed media
on posterboard, each in an edition of four;
each 31" x 49", (78.8 x 124.5 cm); 78" x 44"
(71.1 x 111.8 cm), image
Commissioned by the PATH Corporation
through the Cultural Council Foundation
CETA Artists Project, 1978
WTC
Note: See AKIRA

HAAS, Richard J.
American, born 1936
The Dakota. 1971. Brooke Alexander,
New York
Drypoint (13/40), 19⅞" x 24⅜"
(50.5 x 61.9 cm), image
Acquired 1973
WTC

Haughwout Building, II. 1971
Brooke Alexander, New York
Drypoint (9/40), 25" x 19⅝"
(63.5 x 49.8 cm)
Acquired 1971
WTC

Little Singer Building. 1971
Brooke Alexander, New York
Drypoint (11/40), 35½" x 13½"
(90.2 x 34.3 cm), image
Acquired 1971
WTC

One Bond Street. 1971. Brooke Alexander,
New York
Drypoint (7/40), 21⅞" x 17¾"
(55.6 x 45.1 cm), image
Acquired 1971
WTC

The Ansonia. 1972. Brooke Alexander,
New York
Drypoint (29/60), 25¼" x 16¾"
(64.1 x 42.5 cm), image
Acquired 1973
WTC

The Flatiron Building. 1973
Brooke Alexander, New York
Drypoint (30/60), 41½" x 17½"
(105.4 x 44.5 cm), sheet; 25¼" x 12¾" (64.1
x 32.4 cm), image
Acquired 1973
WTC

HALVORSEN, Francine
American
The Hanging Gardens of Babylon,
Nos. 1–4, from *Rock Paper Scissors*. 1978
Four silkscreen prints with mixed media
on posterboard, each in an edition of four;
each 49" x 31" (124.5 x 78.7 cm), sheet;
44" x 28" (111.8 x 71.1 cm), image
Commissioned by the PATH Corporation
through the Cultural Council Foundation
CETA Artists Project, 1978
WTC
Note: See AKIRA

HARTUNG, Hans
French, born Germany 1904. In Paris since 1935
Black and White
Lithograph (47/75), 24½" x 16¾"
(62.2 x 42.5 cm)
Acquired 1970
WTC

LA 6
Lithograph (44/75), 30" x 22⅛"
(76.2 x 56.2 cm)
Acquired 1970
WTC

LA 30
Lithograph (33/50), 19½" x 25½"
(49.5 x 64.8 cm)
Acquired 1970
WTC

HAYTER, Stanley William
British, born 1901. In Paris 1926–39. In U.S. 1939–50. In Paris since 1950
Symmetry. 1970
Lithograph (28/100), 23¼" x 19"
(59.1 x 48.3 cm)
Acquired 1973
WTC

HEPWORTH, Barbara
British, 1903–1975
Composition. 1969
Color lithograph (44/65), 28" x 19⅝"
(71 x 50 cm)
Acquired 1970
WTC (WTI)

HERBIN, Auguste. French, 1882–1960
Galerie Denise René. (N.d.)
Poster, 47¼" x 30½" (119.4 x 77.5 cm)
WTC

HUNDERTWASSER, Friedensreich
(Friedrich Stowasser)
Austrian, born 1928
Good Morning City! Bleeding Town. 1969
(Series S, 1969–70)
Color serigraph embossed with metal
(3,699/10,000), 33½" x 22" (85 x 56 cm)
Acquired 1970
WTC

Good Morning City! Bleeding Town. 1969
(Series T, 1969–70)
Color serigraph embossed with metal
(3,935/10,000), 33½" x 22" (85 x 56 cm)
Acquired 1970
WTC (WTI)

IKEDA, Masuo
Japanese, born Manchuria 1934. Lives in U.S.
Landscape in the Day
Lithograph (23/55), 26½" x 21½"
(67.3 x 54.6 cm)
Acquired 1970
WTC

Present from the Sky
Lithograph (19/36), 30" x 22¾"
(76.2 x 57.8 cm)
Acquired 1970
WTC

Secret Box
Lithograph (33/36), 26" x 20¼"
(66 x 51.4 cm)
Acquired 1970
WTC

INDIANA, Robert
American, born 1928
American Art
Silkscreen poster (98/100), 35½" x 25½"
(90.2 x 64.8 cm)
Acquired 1971
WTC

JORN, Asger
Danish, born 1914. Lives in Paris and Arbisola Mare, Italy
Untitled plate from *El Circulo de Piedra (Circle of Stone).* 1969. Grafica Uno, Milan
Lithograph, 22¼" x 17¾" (56.5 x 45.1 cm)
Acquired 1970
JFKIA (48)
Note: See ADAMI

KELLER, Germaine
American, born 1938
Untitled, Nos. 1–4, from
Rock Paper Scissors. 1978
Four silkscreen prints with mixed media on posterboard, each in an edition of four;
each 49" x 31" (124.5 x 78.7 cm), sheet;
44" x 28" (111.8 x 71 cm), image
Commissioned by the PATH Corporation
through the Cultural Council Foundation
CETA Artists Project, 1978
WTC
Note: See AKIRA

KELLY, Ellsworth
American, born 1923. In Paris 1948–54
Vivian Beaumont Theater. 1965
H.K.L., Ltd., Boston
Lithograph poster (80/100), 41" x 25¾"
(104.1 x 65.4 cm)
Acquired 1970
WTC

Untitled plate from *Portfolio 9.* 1967
Hollanders Workshop, New York
Lithograph (66/100), 17" x 22"
(43.2 x 55.9 cm)
Acquired 1970
WTC
Note: See FRANCIS

KEPETS, Hugh
American, born 1946
Escape. 1981
Triptych: silkscreen (17/85), 48" x 42"
(121.9 x 106.7 cm)
Acquired 1983
PABT

DE KOONING, Willem
American, born the Netherlands 1904
Clam Digger from *Portfolio 9.* 1967
Hollanders Workshop, New York
Lithograph, (66/100), 17" x 22" (43.2 x 55.9 cm)
Acquired 1970
WTC
Note: See FRANCIS

KOWALSKI, Piotr
Polish, born 1927. Lives in Paris
Untitled plate from *El Circulo de Piedra (Circle of Stone).* 1969. Grafico Uno, Milan
Lithograph, 22¼" x 17¾" (56.5 x 45.1 cm)
Acquired 1970
JFKIA (42)
Note: See ADAMI

KRUSHENICK, Nicholas
American, born 1929
The Minneapolis Institute of Arts: 50th Anniversary Exhibition. 1965
H.K.L. Ltd., Boston
Silkscreen poster (95/100), 35" x 22"
(88.9 x 63.5 cm)
Acquired 1971
WTC

H.K.L. Six-Foot Serigraph. 1968
H.K.L., Ltd., Boston
Serigraph from an edition of 144, 72" x 41"
(182.9 x 104.1 cm)
Acquired 1971
JFKIA (121)

Plates 1–10 from *The Iron Butterfly.* 1968
International Editions, New York, and
Galerie der Speigel, Cologne
Serigraph on ragboard (45/125), each
35½" x 27½" (90.2 x 69.9 cm)
Acquired 1971
JFKIA (93)

New York State Council Award, 1970. 1970
H.K.L., Ltd., Boston
Silkscreen poster (27/144), 35" x 25"
(88.9 x 63.5 cm)
Acquired 1971
WTC

LAING, Gerald
British, born 1936. Lives in U.S.
Pendulum from *Parachutes.* 1964
Richard Feigen Graphics, New York
Serigraph with mixed media from a port-
folio of six plates, 35" x 23" (88.9 x 58.4 cm)
Acquired 1971
JFKIA

Pennon from *Parachutes.* 1964
Richard Feigen Graphics, New York
Serigraph with mixed media (25/75) from
a portfolio of six plates, 35" x 23" (88.9 x 58.4 cm)
Acquired 1971
JFKIA

Plunger from *Parachutes.* 1964
Richard Feigen Graphics, New York
Serigraph with mixed media (25/75) from
a portfolio of six plates, 35" x 23" (88.9 x 58.4 cm)
Acquired 1971
JFKIA

LAM, Wifredo
Cuban, 1902–1982. Worked in France, Spain, and Italy from 1923. Lived in France
Untitled plate from *El Circulo de Piedra (Circle of Stone).* 1969. Grafico Uno, Milan
Lithograph, 22¼" x 17¾" (56.5 x 45.1 cm)
Acquired 1970
JFKIA (40)
Note: See ADAMI

LEVINE, Jack
American, born 1915
Bienvenue (Welcome). 1970
C.F.A. Graphics, New York
Lithograph (52/125), 28½" x 32¾"
(71.8 x 83.2 cm)
Acquired 1970
WTC

Bienvenue (Welcome). 1970
C.F.A. Graphics, New York
Lithograph (103/125), 28¼" x 32¾"
(71.8 x 83.2 cm)
Acquired 1970
WTC

Texas Delegate. (N.d.)
Lithograph (106/120), 21¾" x 27"
(55.2 x 68.6 cm)
Acquired 1971
WTC

Victoria's Jubilee. (N.d.)
Lithograph (62/100), 8¾" x 11⅝"
(22.2 x 29.5 cm), image
Acquired 1970
WTC

A Wedding Gift. (N.d.)
Lithograph (62/100), 8¾" x 11⅝"
(22.2 x 29.5 cm), image
WTC

LICHTENSTEIN, Roy
American, born 1923
Explosion from *Portfolio 9.* 1967
Hollanders Workshop, New York
Color silkscreen (66/100), 17" x 22"
(55.8 x 43.2 cm)
Acquired 1970
NIA
Note: See FRANCIS

LINDNER, Richard
American, born Germany. 1901–1978. To U.S. 1941
Non-Stop. 1967
Triptych, silkscreen poster; each panel,
46" x 34" (116.8 x 86.4 cm)
Acquired 1973
WTC

Tyrone Guthrie: "Arturo Ui." 1969
H.K.L. Ltd. Boston
Silkscreen poster, 29¾" x 19¾"
(75.6 x 50.2 cm)
Acquired 1972
WTC
Note: Designed for Tyrone Guthrie
Theater, Minneapolis

LOVING, Wyn
American
Will You Be Mine, and Other Painful Questions from Old Movies, Nos. 1–4, from
Rock Paper Scissors. 1978
Four silkscreen prints with mixed media on posterboard, each in an edition of four;
each 49" x 31" (124.5 x 78.7 cm), sheet;
44" x 28" (111.8 x 71.1 cm), image
Commissioned by the PATH Corporation
through the Cultural Council Foundation
CETA Artists Project, 1978
WTC
Note: See AKIRA

McGILL, Kurt
American
Impressions of Africa, Nos. 1–4, from
Rock Paper Scissors. 1978
Four silkscreen prints with mixed media on posterboard, each in an edition of four;
each 49" x 31" (124.5 x 78.7 cm); 44" x 28"
(111.8 x 71 cm), image
Commissioned by the PATH Corporation
through the Cultural Council Foundation
CETA Artists Project, 1978
WTC
Note: See AKIRA

MAN RAY
American, 1890–1976. In Paris 1921–40;
1951–76. In U.S. 1940–51
Dancing Figure
Lithograph (21/100), 26⅛" x 19¾"
(66.4 x 50.2 cm)
Acquired 1972
WTC

Two Faces
Lithograph (A.P.), 18½" x 12⅜"
(47 x 81.4 cm)
Acquired 1970
WTC

MIRÓ, Joan
Spanish, 1893–1983. In Paris 1919–40
Blanco no Penetra from *El Circulo de Piedra (Circle of Stone).* 1969
Grafica Uno, Milan
Color lithograph, 22¼" x 17¾"
(56.5 x 45.1 cm)
Acquired 1970
JFKIA (45)
Note: See ADAMI

Série Bleu, II (Blue Series, II).
Color lithograph (14/30), 17½" x 23½"
(44.5 x 59.7 cm)
Acquired 1970
WTC

Le Revenant (The Ghost). 1969
Color lithograph (10/75), 36″ x 25″
(91.4 x 63.5 cm)
Acquired 1971
WTC

MOTHERWELL, Robert
American, born 1915
Automatism A. 1965–66. Hollanders
Workshop, New York
Lithograph (A.P.), 28″ x 21″ (71 x 53.3 cm)
Acquired 1970
WTC

Untitled plate from *Portfolio 9.* 1967
Hollanders Workshop, New York
Lithograph (66/100), 17″ x 22″
(43.2 x 55.9 cm)
Acquired 1970
NIA
Note: See FRANCIS

NEVELSON, Louise
American, born Ukraine 1900. To U.S.
1905.
Dusk in August, from *Portfolio 9.* 1967
Hollanders Workshop, New York
Lithograph with circular embossing (A.P.),
17″ x 22″ (43.2 x 55.9 cm)
Acquired 1970
WTC
Note: See FRANCIS

Dusk in August, from *Portfolio 9.* 1967
Hollanders Workshop, New York
Lithograph with circular embossing
(66/100), 17″ x 22″ (43.2 x 55.9 cm)
Acquired 1970
NIA
Note: See FRANCIS

PEARSON, Henry
American, born 1914
Untitled plate from *Portfolio 9.* 1967
Hollanders Workshop, New York
Lithograph (66/100), 17″ x 22″
(43.2 x 55.9 cm)
Acquired 1970
WTC
Note: See FRANCIS

PETERDI, Gabor
American, born 1915
Red, Red Eclipse. c. 1967. Lublin Graphics,
Greenwich, Connecticut
Etching from an edition of 150 plus 20
artist's proofs, 17¼″ x 23½″
(43.8 x 59.7 cm)
Acquired 1970
JFKIA

Sky and Water. c. 1967. Lublin Graphics,
Greenwich, Connecticut
Etching (48/100), 17¼″ x 23½″
(43.8 x 59.7 cm), image
Acquired 1970
WTC

Sky and Water. c. 1967. Lublin Graphics,
Greenwich, Connecticut
Etching (50/100), 17¼″ x 23½″
(43.8 x 59.7 cm), image
Acquired 1971
WTC

PFAHLER, Georg Karl
German, born 1926
Portfolio of nine untitled plates
Serigraph, each 25″ x 25″ (63.5 x 63.5 cm)
Acquired 1971
JFKIA (118)

PIGNON, Edouard
French, born 1905
Untitled plate from *El Circulo de Piedra
(Circle of Stone).* 1969. Grafica Uno, Milan
Lithograph, 22¼″ x 17¾″ (56.5 x 45.1 cm)
Acquired 1974
JFKIA (43)
Note: See ADAMI

POMODORO, Arnaldo
Italian, born 1926
Untitled. 1968. Collector's Press,
San Francisco
Color lithograph with silver foil from an
edition of 100, 30″ x 22″ (76.2 x 55.9 cm)
Acquired 1970
JFKIA (30)

PORTER, Fairfield
American, 1907–1975
Cityscape, 1969. 1969
Lithograph (84/100), 30″ x 20½″ (76.2 x
52.1 cm)
Acquired 1971
WTC

Broadway. 1972. Brooke Alexander,
New York
Color lithograph (103/125), 29¾″ x 22″
(73.7 x 55.9 cm)
Acquired 1973
WTC

QUINTE, Lothar
German, born 1923
Blue Luna
Serigraph (82/100), 25½″ x 25½″
(64.8 x 64.8 cm)
Acquired 1972
JFKIA (76)

Luna Blue
Serigraph (34/100), 25½″ x 25½″
(64.8 x 64.8 cm)
Acquired 1972
JFKIA (75)

Luna Silver
Serigraph (A.P.), 25½″ x 25½″
(64.8 x 64.8 cm)
Acquired 1972
JFKIA (78)

Silver Luna
Serigraph (80/100), 25½″ x 25½″
(64.8 x 64.8 cm)
Acquired 1972
JFKIA (77)

REBEYROLLE, Paul
French, born 1919
Untitled plate from *El Circulo de Piedra
(Circle of Stone).* 1969. Grafica Uno, Milan
Lithograph, 22¼″ x 17¾″ (56.5 x 45.1 cm)
Acquired 1970
JFKIA (50)
Note: See ADAMI

RIVERS, Larry
American, born 1923
First New York Film Festival. 1964
H.K.L. Ltd., Boston
Lithograph poster (195/250), 46″ x 30″
(116.8 x 76.2)
Acquired 1970
WTC

ROSENQUIST, James
American, born 1933
Circles of Confusion.
Color lithograph and silkscreen (A.P.),
23½″ x 19½″ (59.7 x 49.5 cm)
Acquired 1971
WTC

For Love from *Eleven Pop Artists, III.* 1965
Original Editions, Los Angeles
Color serigraph (70/200), 35″ x 26¼″
(88.9 x 66.7 cm)
Acquired 1971
WTC

Whipped Butter for Eugene Ruchin from
Eleven Pop Artists, II. 1965
Original Editions, Los Angeles
Color serigraph, 30″ x 24″ (76.2 x 61 cm)
Acquired 1971
WTC

SCHEFFELER, Hans York
Blue, Purple, Green Stripes. 1970
Silkscreen (30/75), 25½″ x 25½″
(65 x 65 cm)
Acquired 1972
JFKIA (88)

Yellow and Orange Stripes. 1970
Silkscreen (51/75), 25½″ x 25½″
(65 x 65 cm)
Acquired 1972
JFKIA (89)

SEGAL, George
American, born 1924
New York City Ballet. 1968
H.K.L. Ltd., Boston
Silkscreen poster (70/144), 35″ x 25″
(88.9 x 63.5 cm)
Acquired 1970
WTC

SIQUEIROS, David Alfaro
Mexican, 1896–1974
Mujer (Wife). C.F.A. Graphics, New York
Color lithograph (23/200), 34″ x 26¾″
(86.4 x 67.9 cm)
Acquired 1971
WTC

SNELSON, Kenneth
American, born 1927
New York State Council on the Arts. 1971
H.K.L. Ltd., Boston
Silkscreen poster, 35″ x 25″
(88.9 x 63.5 cm)
WTC

SONENBERG, Jack
American, born Canada 1925
Dimensions, No. 7. 1970
Mixed media, 33⅛″ x 27″ (84.1 x 68.6 cm)
Acquired 1972
JFKIA (90)

SOULAGES, Pierre
French, born 1919
Litho Bleue (Blue Litho). c. 1968
Librairie-Galerie La Hune, Paris
Color lithograph (75/85), 30″ x 22″
(76 x 55 cm), image
Acquired 1970
WTC

Grès (Sandstone). 1969. Lublin Graphics,
Greenwich, Connecticut
Lithograph (38/85), 30½″ x 22⅝″
(77.5 x 57.5 cm)
Acquired 1970
WTC

SOYER, Raphael
American, born Russia 1899. To U.S. 1912
Immigrants from *Self-Revealment and
Memories.* 1969. Lublin Graphics,
Greenwich, Connecticut
Lithograph (133/150), from a portfolio of
12 plates, 15″ x 16″ (38.1 x 40.6 cm), image
Acquired 1970
WTC

The Pier from *Self-Revealment and
Memories.* 1969. Lublin Graphics,
Greenwich, Connecticut
Lithograph (127/150), from a portfolio of
12 plates, 14⅜″ x 14½″ (36.5 x 36.8 cm),
image
Acquired 1970
WTC

STEINBERG, Saul
American, born Romania 1914. To U.S.
1942
Untitled plate from *Portfolio 9.* 1967
Hollanders Workshop, New York
Color lithograph, (66/100), 17″ x 22″
(43.2 x 55.9 cm)
Acquired 1970
WTC
Note: See FRANCIS

SUGAI, Kumi
Japanese, born 1921. To Paris 1952
Plates 1 and 2 from *October: The Silence.*
c. 1970. M'Arte Edizione, Milan
Color lithograph (12/30), 15⅛″ x 11¼″
(38.4 x 28.6 cm)
Acquired 1970
NIA
Note: Portfolio contains poem by
Nathaniel Tarn and second set of the two
plates pulled on Japon nacré paper
(below).

Plates 3 and 4 from *October: The Silence.*
c. 1970. M'Arte Edizione, Milan
Color lithograph (12/106), each
15⅛″ x 11¼″ (38.4 x 28.6 cm)
Acquired 1970
JSTC
Note: See above

TAI, Kwok-Yee
British, born Hong Kong 1947
Untitled, Nos. 1–4, from *Rock Paper
Scissors.* 1978
Four silkscreen prints with mixed media
on posterboard, each in an ediiton of four;
each 49″ x 31″ (124.4 x 78.7 cm), sheet;
44″ x 28″ (11.8 x 71.1 cm), image
Commissioned by the PATH Corporation
through the Cultural Council Foundation
CETA Artists Project, 1978
WTC
Note: *Rock Paper Scissors* installation also
contained ceramic tiles by the artist. See
also AKIRA

TAPIÈS PUIG, Antoní
Spanish, born 1923
Untitled plate from *El Circulo de Piedra
(Circle of Stone).* 1969. Grafica Uno, Milan
Lithograph 22¼″ x 17¾″
(56.5 x 45.1 cm)
Acquired 1970
JFKIA (46)
Note: See ADAMI

VASARELY, Victor
French, born 1908. To France 1930
Poster before Letters. (N.d.). Denise René
Editeur, Paris
Color serigraph (295/300), 27¾″ x 23¼″
(70.5 x 59.1 cm)
Acquired 1970
WTC

Tridimark. (N.d.)
Color serigraph (58/100), 23¼″ x 17¼″ (58.4
x 43.8 cm)
Acquired 1971
WTC

Untitled. (N.d.)
Color serigraph (116/250), 25″ x 24½″ (63.5
x 62.2 cm)
Acquired 1971
WTC (WTI)

Index to Artists in the Collection

COCHRAN, Anna
COUDRAIN, Brigitte
CRANMER, Thomas
CRUZ, Emilio
CUSHMAN, Bruce

DANTE, Giglio
DOLLE, Jean
DONNESON, Seena
DORAZIO, Piero
DORNY, Bertrand
DUBUFFET, Jean
DURAND, Asher

ELLMAN, Emily

FAILLA
FASOLINO
FINI, Leonor
FLORSHEIM, Richard
FOLON, Jean-Michel
FRANK, Mary
FREED, David
FREILICHER, Jane
FUHRMAN, Eather
FUKUI, Nobumitsu

GANTNER, Bernard
GERARDIA, Walter
GIKOW, Ruth
GINSBERG, Elizabeth
GRANT, Gordon
GRAVES, Michael
GREENWALD, Sidney
GUJRAL, Satish
GUNTHER, Max

HARUNOBU, Suzuki
HASEGAWA, Shiochi
HASHIMOTO
HAWKINGS, D.
HAYMSON, John
HAYSLETTE, Max
HEBALD, Milton
HIGA
HILAIRE, Camilla
HINMAN, Charles
HOBART, Roland
HOFFMAN, Arnold
HSIAO

ICHIKAWA
IVES, Norman

JANKOWSKI, Zygmund
JOSDRES, Rob

KELLY, Francis
KELVIN, George V.
KIJNO
KING, Ronald
KIRK, Michael
KNIGIN, Michael
KRASNO, Rodolfo
KWASNIEWSKA, Barbara
KYOSAI

LEBADANG
LETELLIER
LETENDRE, Rita
LEVINSON, Mon
LI T'ANG
LORING, John

LUCAS, Robert
LUNDGREN, Charles

MARKSON, Helena
MAX, Peter
MEHRING
MOTI, Kaiko

NEAL, Otto
NEIMAN, Leroy
NESBITT, Lowell

OLUGEBEFOLA, Ademola

PACKMAN, Alex
PANE, Gina
PAPART, Max
PATTERSON, C.R.
PEEL, Michael
PERESIC, Milan
PERRIN, Brian
PFEIFFER, Werner
POHL, Louis G.
POND, Clayton
PORTER, Katherine
PRIESMAN, Gary

QUANRUD, John

RAYO, Omar
RICE, Brian
ROGERS, James
ROT, Dieter
ROWLAND, Frank

SALZMAN, Rick
SCHLEMM, Betty Lou
SCHWARTZ, Robert
SEARLE, Ronald
SW-GWOI-DON-KWE
SELMAN, Jan
SEQUERI, Robert
SESSIONS, James
SHAHN, Ben
SHEMI, Calman
SHO-SUN
SMIECHOWSKA, Krystina
SOLOVIOFF, Nicholas
SPALATIN, Marko
STAMOS, Theodoros
STOBART, John
STRICKLAND, Steven
SUTTON, Philip
SZLEMKO, Suzanne

TAMAYO, Rufino
THORNTON, Valerie
TONERO, Sergio Gonzalez
TROVA, Ernest
TRUMBULL, Benjamin
TURNER, James
TYSEN, Jan

VON WICHT, Joseph

WAKITA
WATANABE, Sadao
WHEDON, Aida
WILLENBECHER, John

YEWELL, J. Floyd
YOSHIDA, Toshi

ZAO, Wouki
ZEMMER, Yigal
ZOX, Larry

Photo Credits

Photographs for which no credits are given are provided by The Port Authority of New York and New Jersey. Charles Adler, courtesy Seattle Arts Commission, 34. David Allison, front and back covers, frontispiece, 7, 21, 30, 32, 56–57, 60–61, 64, 65, 66 (top left and bottom), 67, 68 (top and bottom left), 69, 70, 71, 72, 73 (top left and right, bottom right), 74, 75, 76, 77, 78 (top and bottom right), 79, 80, 81, 82 (top), 83, 84, 85, 86–87, 88–89 (top), 90, 91, 92–93, 94, 97, 98, 99, 100, 101, 102, 103, 104, 105, 106, 107, 108, 109, 110, 111, 112. Amway Corporation, Ada, Mich., 36 (top). Archives of American Art, Smithsonian Institution, Washington, D.C., 26 (right), 42, 43 (second). Oliver Baker, 38 (right). Courtesy Borgenicht Gallery, New York, 68 (right). Courtesy James Brooks, 45 (right). *Calder: An Autobiography with Pictures*, © 1966, 28–29, 29. Courtesy Leo Castelli Gallery, New York, 52. Chicago Association of Commerce and Industry, 35. Jon Goell, 58, 59. Balthazar Korab, Troy, Mich., 36 (bottom). Dorothy C. Miller, 26 (left). Courtesy The Pace Gallery, New York, 51. Soichi Sunami, 39 (all), 45 (left). Courtesy Whitney Museum of American Art, New York, 55 (bottom).

Committee on Art